Embodying
The God
We Proclaim

God is not a matter for the head but
an experience of the soul; not a theory
to be taught but Presence to be
experienced. pg. 114

Emmaus Productions   Resource Publications, Inc.
P.O. Box 54 Thornleigh   160 E. Virginia Street #290
NSW, 2120 Australia.   San Jose, CA 95112-5876
Phone (02) 9484 0252   Phone (408) 286-8505
Fax (02) 9481 9179   Fax (408) 287-8748

ISBN 0 646 28744 3

Cover Artwork by Dennis Clare
Cover Design by Richard Tabaka
Layout & Typeset by ID Studio, Sydney
Printed in the United States of America
1999

Embodying The God We Proclaim

Ministering As Jesus Did

Monica Brown

Resource Publications, Inc.

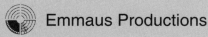
Emmaus Productions

A dedication is an opportunity to formally and publicly thank someone who usually is hidden and unknown, but is in fact, the pillar of inspiration and support of a particular work.

I dedicate this book to
Mary Margaret Brown
(5.8.1925–4.10.1988)

my mother

a big-hearted, spirited woman who taught me by her living more about the values of God's Kingdom and the ministry of Jesus than anyone I have known. My mother embodied the God she proclaimed with passion and commitment. Memories and reminders of what she did and how she ministered in her outreach to all whom she encountered, have inspired my own ministry and my writing here. She is one who by her love was truly recognizable as Jesus' disciple.

I also want to dedicate this book to my father, Francis David Brown, whose love and devotion to my mother and his six children enabled my mother to do what she did in her ministry.

Finally, I dedicate this book to my sisters and brothers, David, Anthony, Josie, Peter and in a special way my twin Elizabeth, and their respective families, as well as my extended family of aunts and uncles who, in very real and practical ways, support my ministry and enable me through their love and belief to continue in my ministry.

C O N T E N T S

INTRODUCTION

E *mbodying the God We Proclaim.* What comes to your mind when you read these words? What meanings do you anticipate will be unearthed in them? What issues and concerns do you expect they will address?

These are some of the questions I have as I attempt to reflect with you on the focus of this book.

What comes to my mind when I ponder this phrase, is people; people who in their being enflesh the mystery of God. *Embodying the God We Proclaim* is about people who in their manner of living and relating not only reflect, but actually make real and accessible, the Presence of God.

Who are these people? They are ordinary people like you and I. They are all of us who seek to live authentically from the depths of our humanity, the mystery of our being in God.

The people who embody the God they proclaim are those of us who struggle to practise in our living what we profess in our words. They are people such as you and I, who are not perfect but genuine in our desire to integrate our beliefs with our actions, our faith with our daily reality.

What if there were one like us who was so authentic in His being that He embodied God in such a way that nothing separated Him from God? What if there were one whose being was so real that there were no contradictions, no inconsistencies, no discrepancies in what He proclaimed about God and what He lived?

What would we experience in one such as this? What would we learn from one so authentic? We would experience nothing less than the Incarnate God! We would learn all that we need to know for life. In Jesus, this One who is like us, we would discover the most credible model for our living and our ministry that we could ever hope to find.

This is why I have sub-titled this book, "Ministering As Jesus Did".

In Jesus' life and ministry we see not only the fullness of the embodiment of God, but we also see the extraordinary impact of His embodiment on the lives of those He encountered. Because of the integrity of what Jesus proclaimed about God and how He lived His humanity, God was validated in Jesus as being living, intimate Presence and the reign of God was truly established.

This book seeks to search out something of the mystery of who Jesus is and what Jesus did so that we who claim to believe in Him might understand a little more of what we are called to embrace in our own lives and in our ministry.

Embodying the God We Proclaim does not attempt to present a theological or scholarly thesis on the life of Jesus. On the contrary, this book presumes a measure of faith and degree of conviction in the heart of the reader that will enable us to ponder the mystery and search out the meanings.

The mystery of Jesus is essentially an experience for the heart, not a theory for the head. Therefore we approach this mystery not with heady notions and theories but with attentive hearts open to the grace of revelation. We turn to Scripture for our guidance here, believing it to be the true Word of God. We ponder it and question it in an attempt to expose ourselves to its rich and sacred revelation.

The objective of this book is to examine the heart of our ministry in the light of Jesus' ministry. Appreciating the purpose of Jesus' ministry and the way He ministered may enable us to evaluate why we do what we do in ministry and how we do it.

Embodying the God We Proclaim raises many questions and issues pertinent to our ministry today. It does not seek to provide answers so much as promote awareness and stimulate discussion on matters that are impacting upon our lives and ministries.

The central concern here is how authentic we are in our ministry. Are we honouring the God of Jesus in the way we proclaim God or are we contradicting, by our actions, our values and our policies, the very nature of the God we are proclaiming?

This raises questions about what motivates our ministry today. Do we have the heart for ministry that Jesus had? More basic than this is the possibility that we may have lost our heart, neglecting it, even casting it aside in our well intentioned pursuit of professionalism and administrative proficiency.

Worse still have we betrayed the heart of our ministry in being less than authentic in our relating, not only to those to whom we minister but to our own colleagues and co-workers? Are we, in our contemporary ministry, becoming less recognizable as Jesus' disciples? Do we really understand what Jesus has done? Are we really honouring His directive to go and do the same?

What effect is the subtle infiltration of the career pursuit and the paper-chase mentality having upon our ministry? Are we being seduced in our ministry by ambition and power? Are we more caught up in providing services than in attending to those whom we encounter? Are the disempowering pressures of the administration and preservation of our institutions and structures locking us into survival and crisis-mode? Are we losing sight of what matters most in our ministry?

Asking these questions in the light of Jesus' ministry challenges us to re-focus not only the motivation of our ministry but the manner in which we minister. Jesus' life and ministry provide us with a model of ministry based on mutual love and friendship. In it Jesus reminds us of forgotten truths and basic values.

9

For this reason much of what is shared in this writing is about how we relate to ourselves, our colleagues and those to whom we minister. There is little if any discussion about programs and activities but extensive soul searching around the basic values of respect, mutuality and justice in our relationships and dealings with others.

By virtue of the nature of its concerns, this book tries to find the balance between the real and the ideal, the strengths and the limitations of our ministry. We are not concerned with perfection but with authenticity. We are not intending to be critical or to judge but to name the issues and articulate the challenges that face us in our ministry today.

There is a deep, passionate hope invested in this book. It is the hope that in evaluating our ministry in the awareness of who Jesus is and what Jesus did, we might recognize that our greatest resource for our ministry is the authenticity of who we are before God. It is a hope that the warmth and sincerity of our humanity will be reclaimed and owned as a leaven for our ministry.

Embodying the God We Proclaim may be a helpful resource for any one involved in ministry, and, in particular, leadership teams, pastoral teams, school staffs and those involved in formation and training in ministry.

The frequent reference in this writing to community is intended to mean the specific community in which you minister and/or the community of your ministry team and colleagues. Your experience of your community is an important backdrop to the reflections offered here. In no way does this book claim to be the final word on the issues and concerns it addresses. It is intended to stimulate discussion and dialogue within your community and to be informed by your experience and insights.

Each chapter of this book has three sections or parts. The first part of each chapter offers a scriptural reflection on Jesus and a specific aspect of His ministry. Part two of each chapter discusses some of the implications of Jesus' ministry in relation to our ministry. Part three of each chapter provides the opportunity for discernment and evaluation.

Part three may be the most important section of each chapter for it offers a series of questions for personal reflection as well as a scriptural meditation. Having encouraged self-reflection and self-evaluation, it then provides a series of questions for the ministry team, whether they be two or three on the pastoral team, or an executive staff or a whole school staff or a formation team. This section concludes with practical suggestions for a ritual and prayer by way of bringing the threads of the group's sharing to a close.

This section in part three is not intended to be a program for evaluation. It merely offers suggestions for focusing on the practical implications, within the local community, of the issues raised in our reflections. It should not be anything more than a guide.

It needs to be noted that the very thought of evaluation can be a threat to some people. The evaluation intended here is in the sense of owning our strengths as well as our limitations. True evaluation will lead to genuine affirmation as well as fair and just challenge. The facilitation of this process of questions and discernment will require some preparation, in as much as the questions and focus may need to be adapted to the circumstances, needs and readiness of the group.

What is imperative here is a real awareness and sensitivity to the members of the group and the issues at hand. Some issues are delicate and need to be dealt with in a sensitive and discerning manner. A team leader may need to be nominated to prepare this process in advance of the group sharing.

The ideas for the ritual are offered, again, merely as a spring-board for your own ideas. The most effective ritual is the one that comes from within the faith sharing.

The music that is suggested for the ritual and prayer is limited to my own collections, simply because I know certain songs relate to the specific focus of the discernment and prayer. However, there are many wonderful hymns and songs by other composers that could serve the same end.

My suggestion in using this book is that time be given for slow reading, quiet pondering and space for discernment. The best insights found in this book will be your own in as much as they draw upon your personal experience and hopefully affirm what you know in light of your own situation.

I recognize that much of what is written here is subjective and therefore may be limited by my own experience. As mentioned earlier, your experience will need to inform what is offered here. So take time to listen to your own experience and your inner movement as you journey with me through these reflections, for your inner movement may well be the stirring of God's Spirit in you.

Finally, I would like to acknowledge those who have supported me in this venture, in particular, my editorial team who have generously worked with me under the pressure of limited time. They are people who are deeply committed to their ministries in pastoral ministry, faith education, spiritual formation, welfare and pastoral care, administration and, not in any way least of all, parenting.

To each of them, Denis O'Brien, Louise and Peter Brown, Gary Bourke, Jenny and Noel Hackett, Sr. Christopher Burrows sgs, Judy and John Mitchell, Br. Graham Neist fms, Rhonda Bourke, Fr. John Ryan ssc, Fr. Michael Walsh cm, Noela Blackmore, Sr. Gerri Boylan sgs, Cathy and Frank Young, Sr. Anna Conway rsm, Fr. Laurie Beath, Mark and Daria Leary, I am truly grateful.

I would like to thank in a special way, Mervyn Melouney, Janine Howell and Maree McLeod for their ever-ready and ever-willing secretarial and administrative assistance.

The final edit of any work is an important task and my mentor and wise friend Sr. Christopher Burrows has been so generous and insightful in assisting me with this. I owe a special thanks to her.

My family and my friends, as always, have supported and encouraged me in so many ways. To each of them I am deeply grateful.

Now, in the Spirit of the One who empowers and enlightens us, let us move on to ponder our questions and search out our meanings.

M. Brown

The Cottage, Thornleigh
June 1996.

CHAPTER I

INCARNATION—HEART OF THE MATTER

PART ONE: SCRIPTURAL REFLECTION

Where does one begin in reflecting upon the Incarnation of Jesus? In the face of such an awesome mystery how does one even attempt to understand, let alone, give expression to the intricacies surrounding the nature of One who is authentically human and truly divine.

At one level the mystery of the Incarnation is incomprehensible, utterly beyond us. At another level, the level of our deepest being, there is a knowing, a sense of what is at the heart of this Incarnational mystery. This knowing is possible because the Spirit of Jesus' own self-utterance gently vibrates and stirs in the soul of each of us, gracing us with a sense of this mystery, enabling us to give expression in some way to the things of God (1 Cor 2:10–12).

Perhaps one begins by acknowledging that one is on holy ground, needing to approach and move reverently within this sacred space, utterly dependent on the movement of grace and the stirrings of the Spirit. Perhaps the beginning point is in listening; listening to that stirring within us, attending to the movement of grace that searches and questions, that wonders and marvels at the meanings and possibilities it senses. So let us ask our questions and ponder our meanings around Jesus.

What was it about Jesus that made such an impact on those He encountered? Who was He? What was He about? Who were the ones drawn to Him and who were the ones who dismissed Him? Why did the people of His day respond as they did to Him?

When Jesus walked this earth wherever He went great crowds would gather and press around Him. Why? What was it about Him that left the crowds in awe of Him? Why did so many seek Him out, follow Him and listen so ardently to His teaching? Why did His teaching make such a deep impression on them? What was it about Jesus that urged people to reach out and touch even the fringe of the garment He wore?

unconditional love - ability to see sincerity.

What caused so many of the poor, the oppressed, the outcast and sinners to associate with Him? And what was it about Jesus that threw His adversaries, the Scribes and the Pharisees, into confusion. What was it about Jesus that confounded them and enraged them to the point of plotting His death? Who was Jesus?

His perfection amplified their imperfection

John was aware of the greatness of Jesus when in commenting at the end of his gospel on all that Jesus did, he wrote, "the world itself, I suppose, would not hold all the books that would have to be written" (Jn 21:25). Prophets, theologians, scholars, philoso-

Jesus caused people to look w/in themselves

16

phers, teachers, artists, dancers, poets, the ordinary woman and man, all of us have asked questions about Jesus.

What were the crowds wondering about Him? What had they sensed in His Presence? What was it about His words, His touch, His way of being? Why did His teaching touch them so much? Was it something about God, something very different, unlike the God presented by their own leaders? Was it something about the way Jesus knew God? Was it something about the way they were coming to know the God of Jesus?

When He touched them it was so genuine a touch that in some extraordinary way, God was enfleshed in His touch. When He laughed and cried, when He was moved with pity, somehow God was there. And when Jesus listened to them, when He spoke, when He embraced, when He comforted them, somehow He made God real and present to them. In one who was like them in so many ways, the people of Jesus' day experienced in Jesus a new sense of God. Sebastian Moore expresses this beautifully,

The 'God' they were now experiencing in the company of Jesus was incomparably more real than the God of traditional religion...Instead of a God who was remote and enigmatic, invoked in a formal way, there was a loving presence in everything, it brought people together; it promoted human flourishing everywhere. (1)

Jesus was the human springtime in the midst of their winter. Jesus made God real and relevant, touchable and seeable, in and through His self-giving from the depths of His being.

But how believable was this God of Jesus? Could this God be trusted? Could Jesus Himself be trusted? If the God they had come to experience in Jesus was real and believable, then what did that say about Jesus? What had they learnt about Jesus Himself through the experience of God they had encountered in Him?

Perhaps they sensed something about His authenticity. Perhaps they had come to appreciate that somehow, beyond their imagining, Jesus was God's most authentic human self-expression. But what did that mean to them? If Jesus was anything less than authentic, if He were merely play-acting being human, if He were puppet-like in His being, then the God they had sensed to be so real in Him would have to be less than believable in the claims of love which God enfleshed for them in Jesus.

What would it mean to doubt Jesus' authenticity? Surely it would be the ultimate disrespect for and disregard of God's self-initiated and self-confessed love of our humanity. More than that, if Jesus were less than real and genuine in His human enfleshment then the truest and surest hope we have of salvation is deeply flawed and seriously suspect.

In the humanity of Jesus we get a glimpse of the profound reverence God has for us, when we appreciate that God freely became one with us, embraced our human condition so completely that God became flesh and lived amongst us. Do we really appreciate this mystery? The authenticity of Jesus' humanity, not only bears witness to God's reverence and love for us, but is the actual enfleshment and human expression of that love and reverence.

The fear for many of us may be that if we take Jesus' humanity seriously then surely we are diminishing His divinity. How could He possibly be human *and* divine?

In attempting to appreciate the fullness of Jesus' human nature we are at the same time honouring the glory of His divinity since only God could embody such authentic humanity as was enfleshed in Jesus. Not even Abraham and Moses, none of the great prophets could surpass the greatness of Jesus. In rebuking the Scribes and the Pharisees who refused to believe, Jesus Himself said, "there is something even greater here than Solomon" (Mt 12:38–42). Indeed there was nothing less than God!

But how could this be? Jesus was one like them and yet there was something more about Him. They sensed it but could not name it, they felt it but could not explain it. There was something in the way He lived, something in the way He related that was more than they knew.

Recognizing that Jesus was one like them was to acknowledge that Jesus was gifted with the freedom to choose and decide. In being human Jesus had the freedom to make choices. In accepting this in Jesus we therefore recognize that, in making His choices in life, there would have been times when He was tempted, like you and I, to choose a way that was not God's way.

When we talk about Jesus being tempted we no doubt go to the synoptic gospels for the account of His temptation in the wilderness (Mt 4:1–17). This magnificent account of Jesus' struggle with His own being is often preached as a once-and-for-all experience that occurred for forty days and forty nights, after which Jesus was rid of all temptation and washed His hands of that aspect of His humanity.

If Jesus was authentic in His capacity to choose and make decisions then it is highly unlikely that His experience in the wilderness was a once-and-for-all time experience. On the contrary, given His authenticity Jesus' capacity for and experience of temptation would have been so genuine that it surely would have remained with Him as part of His human experience right to the moment of His death.

Let us consider here what we mean by tempted. To be tempted implies firstly the capacity to make choices, to know right from wrong and good from bad. It means there is a capacity, to varying degrees according to one's overall human development, to choose between the pullings of the archetypal opposites at the depths of the human heart that wrestle for our attention as we struggle for wholeness.

Many of these opposites are poetically named in Ecclesiastes 3: the pull between love and hate, resentment and forgiveness, selfishness and self-giving, power and powerlessness, laughter and tears, building up and breaking down, holding on and letting go, living and dying, heaven and earth, God's way and our way, human and divine.

My sense is that Jesus knew it all, not just in the wilderness alone but, in a special way, in His relationships. If Jesus was truly human then temptation was there, no doubt very often, in the way He responded to people and situations. Let us take some time here to reflect upon a few situations wherein Jesus may have been tempted to choose another way.

The first incident I would like to reflect upon is one that has always struck me as being out of character for Jesus. It is the encounter with the pagan woman who begged Jesus to heal her daughter who was tormented by a devil. In Matthew's account (Mt. 15:21–28), Jesus seems determined to ignore this woman despite her shouting and pleading. She begs Him to take pity on her and her daughter. Matthew reports that Jesus "answered her not a word" (15:23). So strong was Jesus' disregard of the woman, the disciples had to plead with Him to attend to her.

One has a sense of holding one's breath waiting to see what will happen, while grappling with the possibility that Jesus just might reject this woman and her plea. Not only does Jesus seem unconcerned about the woman, He appears to be utterly disrespectful of her, referring to her and her child as "dogs", a well-known Jewish term for pagans.

The woman's quick and skilful response about how even the house-dogs are able to eat scraps from the master's table seems to trigger a shift in Jesus. What went on in His mind and heart? Up to this point Jesus was not only choosing to refuse this woman but to judge her as others did.

Jesus' self-justification for refusing to help her because He was sent only to the "House of Israel" (15:25) reveals something of His deep sense of mission to the people of God. But somehow in that moment, in the face of this woman and her plea, Jesus is challenged to review His sense of mission and even His sense of who the people of God might be. His choice here is to deepen His understanding of His mission and widen His perspective of who God's people are, or to continue to dismiss this woman as one who is outside the grace of God's Kingdom.

For some reason once He became engaged with this woman Jesus changed. How He chooses to respond to her now is virtually the opposite of His initial response to her. He not only attends to her need by healing her daughter but He affirms her now as a woman of great faith.

I do not claim in any way to know the mind and heart of Jesus, but there is no doubt here that Jesus chose the way of God in a situation where He may have been tempted to choose the way of judgement and rejection and in doing so refuse God's healing power to all God's people.

The second example of how Jesus may have been tempted to choose another way is an interesting one because of its timing. It is the healing of the epileptic demoniac in Mark's gospel (Mk.9:14–29).

All three synoptic writers place this incident immediately after the Transfiguration of Jesus. Such consistency of the sequence of events in the gospels is not common. However, in this case, it is when Jesus literally comes down from the mountain that He is immediately confronted by a large crowd arguing with His disciples. When they see Jesus, the focus is shifted to Him. He tries to get to the heart of the problem. A man explains that his son is possessed and when he asked Jesus' disciples to cure his son the disciples could not cast out the destructive spirit.

It is the strength of Jesus' reply that is surprising here, especially in light of the Transfiguration experience. Jesus calls them faithless

21

and in what seems to be utter exasperation He asks how long He must be with them. Even more than exasperated Jesus goes further and asks how long must He "put up" with them (9:19). Is Jesus frustrated? Has He had enough? Is He being patronizing in His comments?

The crowds and disciples, except the three who witnessed the Transfiguration, do not know what Jesus has experienced on the mountain top. But Jesus knows. Is He still caught up in the bliss of that experience? Is He experiencing the pull between heaven and earth? Is Jesus frustrated and discouraged about His mission; about their inability to understand?

At this point of frustration Jesus has the opportunity to throw up His hands and walk away from it all. The fact that He doesn't is not because He was any less human than you or I. The fact that He chooses the way of God and brings about healing and reconciliation in this incident, despite His own human emotion and desires, indicates how deeply Jesus was centred in God and how committed He was in establishing the reign of God.

The last example I would like to reflect upon is very different from these previous examples. It is the anointing of Jesus' feet at Bethany. (Jn 12:1–8)

According to John's version of this incident, Jesus had previously raised Lazarus from the dead and a dinner had been given in Jesus' honour at Lazarus' house. Jesus is surrounded by His friends and disciples, and is relaxed and enjoying it immensely.

While Martha waited on them at table, Mary came and anointed Jesus' feet with an expensive oil and then wiped His feet with her hair. Now, in John's account, it is Judas Iscariot who is indignant at the waste of money that could have been used for the poor. In the accounts given by Mark and Matthew the anointing occurs in Simon the leper's house and there, several of the disciples were indignant about the wastefulness (Mk 14:3–9), (Mt 26:6–13).

Regardless of the inconsistencies concerning the place and the objectors, it is the consistency of the objection and Jesus' response to it that is of interest here.

The objection seems quite valid, after all Jesus has taught them to be aware of the poor. Perhaps He has taught them too well since their objections seem to have put Jesus in an embarrassing and delicate situation. Jesus is faced with a number of choices here.

If Jesus agrees with the objection and dismisses Mary He may offend someone He genuinely loves. Furthermore, if Jesus upholds the objection He loses the opportunity to be nurtured by this woman who obviously loves Him. Is it possible that like you and me, Jesus needed and longed for some tender nurturing? The experience for Jesus of having his feet massaged, would surely have been a rare pleasure for Him. He is faced now with an objection that could mean the end of this no doubt rare opportunity for Jesus to receive something out of love from another.

But not to object could leave Jesus open to misunderstanding and the judgement by His friends and disciples of being inconsistent and, at worst, hypocritical in allowing Himself to be pampered while the poor suffer.

It is an interesting and hard choice for Jesus. Some might consider that in choosing to allow Mary to continue anointing His feet, Jesus did give into temptation. Others might consider that He failed to choose God's way by being insensitive to the poor. Others again might sense that Jesus did choose God's way in choosing the way of love and nurturing. Whatever one's sense of this incident, there is no doubt that Jesus was faced with real temptation and hard choices between God's way and the way of selfishness and sin.

To say that Jesus was without sin is to say that He always chose the way of God, that He never turned away from God in any choice He made.

It is not as if we had a high priest incapable of feeling our weakness with us; but we have one who has been tempted in every way that we are, though He is without sin... (Heb 4:15)

That's the difference between Jesus and us. He never chose anything less than God nor any way other than God's way. But, as the text from Hebrews reminds us, Jesus was capable of experiencing all that we experience. Jesus was tempted and He would have struggled, at times beyond our imagining, to choose God's way. Perhaps that's what they saw in Him, His fidelity to God's way?

What had God done in one so much like them? What had been God's intention? If Jesus were truly one like them, then why did they sense so much more in Him? What had God done in this One who was truly human and yet, really divine? And why? Why had God done all that God did in Jesus?

God chose, it seems, to assume the humanity that was considered by the world to be foolish and weak. God embraced the human spirit that the powerful, proud and ambitious failed to recognize as godly. It raises many questions for us about in whose face we look for God and in whose face we recognize God?

The humanity that God assumed was hidden and unnoticed, so like the ordinary, simple, humble, powerless, not even with "looks to attract" (Is 53:1–3)! Only those who could see with the eyes of their hearts and hear with the ears of their hearts could recognize in one so like themselves the Presence of their God.

So genuine was God's dwelling amongst God's people that within the depths of their struggle, their pain and oppression they experienced the Presence of God. Where the God of their tradition had been proclaimed by their religious leaders to be distant, aloof and removed from their human mess, and even judgemental of it, the God made flesh in Jesus was one *with* them in their human plight.

Rather than judge their human story this God of Jesus blessed it. You who are poor in spirit, gentle, pure in heart, blessed are you!

You who mourn, who thirst for right, who show mercy, who seek peace, who are persecuted in the cause of right, blessed are you (Mt.5:1–12)!

What God had done in Jesus was to make real and immediate the reign of God's Kingdom. In the face of human heartache and struggle Jesus healed, reconciled and forgave. Jesus affirmed the broken spirit and restored dignity. Jesus gave new hope and new meaning, not as One who was separate from human concerns, but as One who would embrace all human suffering in His own wounding (Is 53:4–5).

In Jesus the stuff of our human suffering and brokenness becomes the holy ground and sacred meeting place of God's transforming love.

Believing this requires a deeper acceptance in us of the authenticity of Jesus' Incarnation. To accept anything less than real humanity in this one who is truly divine is to question the authenticity of all that Jesus lived and died for. Anything less than real humanity in Jesus makes the Passion of Jesus nothing more than a human drama rather than human *experience*, His death simply an exceptional performance rather than *complete utter self-surrender*, and His Resurrection a shrewd myth rather than the climactic *transcendence of humanity* and the *ultimate triumph of life* for all time.

What God has done in and through Jesus is affirm our dignity and bless our humanity. God has given us in Jesus, a new way of being, a new way of living and even a new way of dying.

PART TWO: IMPLICATIONS

1. A NEW IMAGE OF GOD

Perhaps one of the most challenging implications for us today, in relation to the mystery of Jesus' incarnation, is the experience of God that Jesus enfleshed.

We have just considered how Jesus revealed a new experience of God for the people of His day. It was new in as much as it was the fullest, richest and most authentic experience of God they had known. It was new in the sense that it made real and accessible the God for whom they had longed, but who, in their established religion, appeared to be distant from them. So genuine was the God Jesus enfleshed that it exposed and challenged the hypocrisy and religious manipulation of their own religious leaders.

This challenges us to examine our own image of God. Is the face of God that Jesus enfleshed the face of the God we know and present to those whom we encounter?

This question has no relevance to anyone who does not claim to believe in the God of Jesus. But to those of us who struggle with our faith in God, the question might be critical. Is the God we believe in the God of Jesus? If the God of our believing is the God of Jesus then does our God bear the same image and likeness of Being that Jesus enfleshed?

As we look at the life of Jesus do we recognize our God? If so what is the image of God we embrace in Jesus? If not, then who is the God we believe in? How is that God different from the God of Jesus?

Such questions are critical for us who have the awesome and privileged responsibility of ministering in Jesus' name. There is no doubt that in our society today, and sadly in some of our faith communities, there are many false Gods being proclaimed, just as there were in Jesus' day. We need to examine our hearts and our lives in search of the God of Jesus. Having come into the experience of that God, we need to embrace God and honour the nature of our God in the way we proclaim God.

The God revealed in Jesus is beautifully exposed in the way Jesus ministered. As we journey through the gospel accounts of Jesus' ministry let us seek out the Spirit and Heart, the Presence and Being of the God whom Jesus enfleshed, so that we may recognize more deeply the God we are called to proclaim.

2. A NEW SELF IMAGE

What has God done in Jesus? God has blessed us in our humanity and affirmed the dignity of our being. What are the implications of this for each of us?

If we believe that God fully embraced and embodied our human nature in Jesus then what does that say to us about God's perception of our humanity? Does it suggest to us in any way that God sees some worth in our human being? Is it possible that God actually perceives a beauty and a dignity at the core of our being that we ourselves cannot even imagine?

Is it possible that, even in the face of our worst sin, our deepest refusal of God, that God sees in the mess of our brokenness, a spirit worthy of love; a love that is so unconditional that it is capable of empowering, healing, and restoring dignity? Is it possible that you and I could matter so much to God?

The Incarnation of Jesus not only bears witness to the worth that God has for us but it translates into flesh the breadth and depth of the love that impassions the sense of God's worth for us.

How deeply does this theology penetrate our understanding and our believing? Does it enlighten the dim image we have of ourselves? Does it thaw out something of the cold and hardened attitudes we have about ourselves? Does the depth of God's reverence and love for us challenge the way we see ourselves and the way we value our being?

Our difficulty in valuing ourselves and the dignity of our being may be a significant factor in the struggle we may have in accepting the human authenticity of Jesus' Incarnation.

If one were to perceive little worth and value in being human, then the notion of God choosing to fully embrace our humanity may seem shocking. But if we were able to perceive humanity as God does, as being precious and honourable, as bearing God's own image and likeness, then perhaps God's total embrace of our humanity is nothing less than profound reverence. Perhaps the mystery of Incarnation is the mystery at the heart of our own being.

Accepting the human authenticity of Jesus' Incarnation and, with it, God's reverence for us, may require a shift in our attitudes towards ourselves and a conversion of heart.

The conversion that is required...is not always, exclusively, an intellectual change of mind, the graduation to a better theology; it may rather be a healing of the heart concerning the value of one's own humanity in the face of God and the tribunal of one's self. (2)

If we are unable to change our self-vision and self-perception, then we will be refusing the most powerful and sincere affirmation of our being. More than that, we will be refusing the greatest opportunity we will ever have to grow, to reach our potential. And what is our potential? We see it in Jesus; to bear the image and likeness of our God most authentically. Sebastian Moore explains the nature of our refusal in this matter,

What we are refusing is...some fullness of life to which God is impelling us and which our whole being dreads. Some unbearable personhood, identity, freedom, whose demands beat on our comfortable anonymity and choice of death. Further something that at

root we are, a self that is ours, yet persistently ignored in favour of the readily satisfiable needs of the ego. (3)

In accepting the mystery of Incarnation we are challenged to accept reverently, a new self-being in God. Essentially this is a challenge for us to embrace our own incarnation. In accepting this challenge we strive to see our sin and our brokenness as the sacred meeting ground and blessed occasion of God's transcending grace in us.

What God has done to us and within us is what Jesus did to those He encountered on this earth. Let us notice in our forthcoming chapters how Jesus responds in the gospels to the *one with whom we identify*, the one who is perhaps poor, oppressed, blind or unclean, crippled, broken or judged. Having identified ourselves with them, let us be aware that Jesus' response to them is how God responds to us.

The implication of the Incarnation is that we see and treat ourselves and each other as God does. Any other perception may imply that God's intention in the Incarnation of Jesus has been missed by us.

3. A NEW WAY OF LIVING More

Jesus' life and ministry was a radical and prophetic statement to the people of His day that there was another way of being with self and with others; there was another way of seeing and judging and there was clearly another way of acting.

What was this new way of Jesus? It was the way of "more"; the understanding that there is more than what meets the eye. There is, in Jesus' way of living, more, for example, to the sinner than the sin, more to love than loving only friends, and more to forgiveness than forgiving only those who forgive us. There is more to being last than being first, more to giving than just giving from our surplus, and more to true worship than parading our good deeds. And there is, ultimately, more to life than death! In His living, Jesus turned it all around, upside down and inside out.

The cries of injustice in our society today, the struggle for dignity and true quality of life, challenge us to model a new way of being. The challenge is to proclaim by our lives that there is something more than the little, the less, the selfish and unjust ways of our society and sometimes even of our Church.

The new way of living that Jesus gave us is the way of paradox. For us to live the way of Jesus is to recognize and own that the way of God is not our way and the thoughts of God are not our thoughts (Is 55:8–9).

As we reflect on Jesus' way, as presented in the gospel accounts in the following chapters, let us be aware of what pulls within us, for that pull will be our invitation to embrace the way of Jesus more fully.

PART THREE: RESPONDING TO THE IMPLICATIONS

Personal Synthesis:

1. What feelings do these reflections stir in you?

2. What issues and concerns do they raise for you?

3. What insights would you like to add to these reflections?

4. When have you felt blessed and affirmed by God? How did you experience God's blessing and affirmation? In what way do you struggle to embrace the image God has of you? What can you do to attend to this?

5. In what way do you feel the pull in your life, between God's way and your own way? Why do you experience this pull?

   What prevents you from choosing the way of God? How can you address this?

6. When have you lived the "more" that Jesus calls us to live? How have you been able to do this? In what particular area of your life do you feel challenged to live the "more" of Jesus' way? What draws you to do so? What prevents you from embracing it? What can you do that may enable you to deal with this challenge?

Scripture Reflection:

Take some quiet time to reflect upon the following text.

"The Word Was Made Flesh..." (Jn 1:1–5, 9–14, 16–18)

• What is it about this Incarnational mystery that leaves you with a sense of awe? What is it about this mystery that you find most challenging?

• Take time to give expression, in word, image, movement or song to this mystery of Incarnation in your life.

Jesus = acceptance: His Father's will; death on a cross; expressions of love; other's ignorance; sinners, lepers. He took the world as it is.

For Group Sharing:

• Allow the group time to connect and gather before you begin discussing these questions. It is important to be aware of people's energy and readiness for what is to follow. In light of this, it may be more appropriate to be selective with these questions or even to disregard them and find another way for your group to respond to the implications.

1. Each share in some way with the group something of your own personal synthesis of these reflections.

2. What questions, concerns and issues do these reflections raise for you as a ministry team within your community?

3. What image of God do you present to your community? How does this God resemble the God of Jesus? *whenever I manage to put myself aside I present God. It is only because of God that I am able to forgive, to demonstrate charity.*

Fr. Greg ← 4. Who are the individuals in your community who reflect the human face of God? What are the factors that make it difficult for you to recognize the face of God in others? *Our culture of violence and selfishness causes me to categorize people.*

5. What would God bless and affirm in you as a team? What efforts and initiatives within your ministry would God delight in? *To have same respect and humility w/ strangers that I do w/ friends.*

6. How do you as a ministry team and as a community live the "more" that Jesus calls us to live? In what areas of your ministry do you feel challenged to live more fully the way of Jesus? What are some initiatives you can implement that may enable you to address this?

7. Take some time of quiet to review what has been shared. Discern as a team something that you can set in motion or further develop that would expose your community more deeply to the mystery of the Incarnation in their lives.

RITUAL AND PRAYER

* The following are suggestions that may assist you in bringing your sharing to prayer. They are only suggestions and should not be considered in any other way. It would be better to create your own prayer and ritual than to rely on something that comes from outside your sharing.

Suggestions:

1. Create a sacred space and atmosphere of quiet and stillness within the group. Soften lights if necessary and play some quiet background music. Give people time to focus. Light a candle and place the Word and or relevant symbols within the centre of the group. Try to integrate into the sacred space something that has come from your sharing. Ensure that people are able to see the sacred focus, that they are comfortable and ready to enter into the prayerful spirit of this time.

2. Plan and prepare a ritual that will enable your team to give expression to the mystery of the Incarnation of Jesus. Perhaps a litany that could come from the group's quiet reflection on the Word of God. Perhaps each team member could contribute a word or phrase that would complete the invocation of the litany. For example, "Jesus, Incarnate God who...." A suitable response to each invocation could be recited or sung by the group. There may be a way of integrating into this litany a gesture or an image.

3. The following scripture may be appropriate:
    John 1:1–5, 9–14, 16–18

4. Some of the following songs may be helpful (please refer to page 191 for location of songs):
    Gather Us O God (ARH)
    So Much More (ARH)
    Lead Me Guide Me (BUH)

This Is Your Way (COJ)
We Sing Your Praise (ARH)
To The Glory Of God (BUH)

5. At the conclusion of your prayer share a meal or a drink or something that will enable people to celebrate and or debrief.

CHAPTER 2

EMBODYING THE GOD WE PROCLAIM

PART ONE: SCRIPTURAL REFLECTION

Our reflections in the previous chapter were an attempt to search out something of the mystery of the Incarnation of Jesus and its implications for us. With this as background we will now focus our attention on how Jesus ministered and the impact of His ministry, not only on those whom He personally encountered but on all those who heed the call to follow Him. Our hope is that we may be able to glean some insights into Jesus' ministry which may enable us to evaluate our own efforts to honour Jesus' directive to go and do the same (Jn 13:15).

As mentioned briefly in our first chapter, Jesus had an extraordinary impact upon the individuals and crowds whom He encountered. For some, such as the fishermen, the tax collectors, the sinner, the outcast, the sick and the needy, Jesus had a profound and life-giving impact.

As a result of what was sacredly held in their hearts and reverently uttered upon their lips about Jesus, the gospel writers have recorded: that Jesus' reputation rapidly spread everywhere (Mk 1:28), people from all around would come to Him (Mk 1:45), everyone was filled with awe (Lk 7:16) and were all astounded by Him (Lk 5:26). There is no doubt that for some, Jesus made a deep heartfelt impression. Because of Him their lives would never be the same.

But for others, such as the Scribes and the Pharisees, the uphold-ers of the Law and the institution, the devout, the Sadducees, the Zealots and the politically ambitious, Jesus had a most disturbing impact. For these Jesus was frustrating, challenging and threaten-ing. He left them feeling so indignant and confounded that they plotted against him (Lk 4:28–30).

Jesus was for these an obstacle to be overcome, a radical idealist who had to be suppressed, a rabble rouser who had to be dealt with. Unable to open their hardened hearts or their stubborn minds to Jesus, these were the ones who looked for a way to destroy Him (Mk 3:1–6).

One way or another Jesus made an impact, a deep and lasting impression. And yet in some way He disappointed everyone. Whatever their personal impression of Jesus, He was one who could not be possessed or dominated, owned or held on to by anyone. Nor could Jesus be dismissed, let go of or forgotten. It was not that Jesus was elusive or an enigma, so much that He was totally present, deeply focused, genuinely open, radically free and utterly centred in God.

Jesus was single-minded and single-hearted. He had a burning desire for one thing only, a passionate will for one purpose, to establish the reign of God, to proclaim the year of God's favour (Lk 4:19).

What did this mean to Jesus? In a very real and practical way it meant that the blind would see, the deaf would hear, the lame would walk and the dead would be given new life (Lk 7:22–23). For Jesus, establishing the reign of God was concerned with liberating captives whatever their form of captivity. It was concerned with unburdening the spirits of those who were downtrodden and restoring their dignity. The reign of God, for Jesus, was about proclaiming to the poor, whatever their poverty might be, the good news that they were the blessed and favoured of God (Lk 4:16–22). Ministry for Jesus was about life—the fullness of God's life. It was about lifting people up, affirming their dignity and showering them with God's favour. Ministry for Jesus was about making God's presence immediate and real in the life experience of all those whom He encountered.

[handwritten marginalia: "→ what is the definition of this?"]
[handwritten marginalia: "More than direct aid (which he also gave at times.) He gave hope to those w/ none, what about those in power who had the means to end the poverty? How did Jesus try to △ them?"]

Jesus' ministry was not concerned with overthrowing structures, organizations and institutions, or setting up groups and steering committees, or administering programs and activities. Jesus simply attended to the now and related to those in His midst. Out of this miracles happened, structures were transformed, groups did gather, communities were formed and in them rituals and activities that had never been so life-giving were established.

When we reflect upon the gospel accounts of Jesus' ministry it appears that His ministry was about relationship. Jesus had an extraordinary ability *to meet people where they were*, physically and spiritually, to connect in some way with their reality and *attend to them*. In attending to them He became *engaged with* them, *relating to* them in a spirit of mutuality and love and in that engagement *God was enfleshed*. The Good News of the reign of God was proclaimed by Jesus in *response to and in relationship with* the life experience of all those He encountered.

One of the most beautiful examples of this model of Jesus' ministry is the Emmaus story (Lk 24:13–35) which will be addressed in our last chapter. For now, however, let us consider a few of the many other examples of how Jesus actually ministered.

The first encounter for our consideration is the story of the Samaritan woman at the well (Jn 4:1–30). Usually this gospel is proclaimed from the perspective of evangelization. While evangelization is certainly a significant feature of this encounter, it is not the only perspective from which this story can be appreciated. Evangelization of this Samaritan woman and her community does not occur until after the woman at the well experiences Jesus as the One who knows her story, accepts her in it and, in response to it, reveals Himself to be the Messiah for whom she longs. It is from this perspective of relationship that I would like to reflect upon this story.

The gospel indicates that the woman in this encounter is unable to maintain relationships (4:18). No doubt she was a woman who knew all the heartache and restlessness that is associated with broken and failed relationships.

Jesus meets this woman in her reality, doing what she does everyday, drawing water from the well. He makes contact with her by asking her for a drink. In seeking such hospitality from this Samaritan woman, Jesus disregards the traditional antagonism between Jews and Samaritans, as well as the criticism He would receive for associating with a woman in public. Aware of all this the woman is confused and tells Him so. Jesus responds to her by telling her that He can give her water that would quench her thirst and satisfy her restless spirit forever.

Here we see how Jesus connects with her. He engages her attention in what appears to be her immediate need of water and once she is engaged with Him, He begins to explore with her, her real need. Jesus is remarkably skilful in the way He engages this woman in reflection on her life.

By challenging her to call her husband and return with him, Jesus gives the woman the opportunity to own her story. We know what happens from this point. Jesus reveals His knowledge of this woman's life. He lets her know that He is aware of her most personal struggle. Perhaps to take attention from herself the woman's comment about Jesus being a prophet leads them into discussion about true worship of God.

All of this is leading to the climactic disclosure of Jesus' own truth. The woman indicates that she will learn everything she needs from the Messiah. At this point Jesus reveals Himself to her, "I who am speaking to you, I am He." (4:26).

Do we appreciate what has happened in this encounter? Jesus engages Himself with a woman who is judged by the Jewish leaders to be not only religiously unworthy but morally suspect. Jesus meets her right in the heart of her territory and in the stark reality of her life experience. He not only reveals to her His knowledge of her life, but He indicates His acceptance of her by revealing His own deepest truth, "I am He" (4:26); I am the One you are waiting for, the Messiah, the One who will reveal everything to you.

Jesus does not condemn this woman, nor demand that she set about putting her life in order. He accepts her in her brokenness. He establishes a relationship of mutuality with her by revealing Himself to her in response to her story.

The gospel account does not indicate any further exchange between Jesus and the woman after His self-revelation just before the disciples returned from buying food. However, I wonder what was happening in this woman in response to all that she had experienced with Jesus? She had come to the well as she had done every other day, probably expecting nothing more than to fill her water jar. Instead of getting water she had met her God, the One whom she declared to the people in her town to be "a man who has told me everything I've ever done…"(4:29).

This declaration in itself reveals so much about Jesus' ministering in this encounter. It was in the intimacy of sharing this woman's story and of His own self-disclosure that Jesus made God real and immediately present, not only to this woman, but to many others from her community. It is a beautiful model of how Jesus ministers through relationship.

Let us move on to consider another example of how Jesus ministers. The account from Luke's gospel about the Widow of Nain (Lk 7:11–17) reveals much about the ever present and sensitive spirit of Jesus.

The crowds had gathered around the burial procession of a young man who had died, leaving his widowed mother alone. Jesus seems to be observing what is happening, taking it all in. He notices the grief of the boy's mother. There is no indication from the gospel that Jesus was urged by anyone other than Himself and the sadness He felt for the widow, to do what He did. Jesus went to her and comforted her because He "felt sorry for her" (7:13).

In comforting her Jesus connected with the woman in her heartache. He was so deeply moved by her situation that He raises the widow's son from the dead. Again there is nothing to suggest that Jesus was asked by the boy's mother or anyone else to restore the boy to life. It seems to be a spontaneous response by Jesus in the face of human suffering.

A further testimony to Jesus' deep sensitivity to this widow is that Jesus actually "gave the boy to his mother" (7:16). This gesture seems to return the focus of this encounter to the grieving widow.

Jesus gave her nothing tangible, yet it was more valuable than the water she came to get. What was it, do I have it, & how can I share it?

It is her heartache that appears to be more the concern of Jesus in this encounter. It suggests that Jesus was honouring the widow's need and, in so doing, restored and renewed her own life as much as the life of her son.

Naturally everyone was filled with awe. Their conclusion was that "God has visited His people" (7:17). And this is the heart of the matter. Jesus' ability to meet people as they are, to connect with them and attend to their needs, in this case with such loving sensitivity, is precisely how Jesus enfleshed God in the midst of human suffering.

Our last example of how Jesus ministered is quite different from these previous examples and less obvious in revealing Jesus' pattern of encounter, attending, engagement and embodiment. It is the evangelical discourse from Matthew's gospel (Mt 5–7).

Seeing the crowds Jesus went up the hill, sat down and began to teach them, "Happy are you"...was how He began to address them. We all know the Beatitudes. They are so familiar to us that often their impact is not realized. Let us look afresh at this discourse in light of Jesus' model of ministry.

How does Jesus deal with such a crowd? How does He connect with so many? Perhaps for awhile He just looks at the crowd gathering. Perhaps He sees faces in the crowd, faces that He has encountered before and no doubt many new faces. But Jesus sees more than faces. Somehow He sees beyond the faces into the eyes and hearts and spirits of the individuals who give shape to this crowd.

Jesus connects with this crowd by being present to them, aware of them and fully focused on them. He indicates in the way He addresses them that He is aware of them and their reality. He calls out to the spirit of each of them,

Happy are you who are poor in spirit... you who are gentle... you who mourn... you who hunger and thirst for what is right... you

who are merciful... you who are poor in heart, you who are peace-makers, you who are persecuted and abused... (Mt 5:3–12).

We can imagine the surprise of each of them as they hear Him name their reality; the surprise at being noticed by Him, at being addressed, somehow in a most intimate way by Him, even in the thick of a crowd! Perhaps some even felt embarrassed or vulnerable in the Presence of One who seemed to know their struggle so deeply.

Having connected with them in this way, Jesus then affirms them in who they are. In so doing He attends to them by reassuring them that their day will come, that it will all turn around for them. He says to them,

Happy are you ...for the Kingdom of heaven is yours..., the earth shall be your heritage..., you shall be comforted..., you shall be satisfied..., you will have mercy shown you..., you shall see God..., you shall be called children of God..., the kingdom of heaven will be yours..., your reward will be great in heaven... (Mt 5:3–12).

Jesus declares them happy and blessed, affirming them in their reality, turning their human struggle into the sacred passage through which they enter God's Kingdom. Jesus goes on to make it very clear that they are the ones who matter to God. He calls them "salt of the earth and light of the world" (5:13–14)! What an extraordinary thing to say to those whom the institution condemns as unworthy outcasts and sinners! Jesus affirms their dignity before God. No wonder they loved Him! He gave them a sense of their own worth and made holy all that they struggle with.

Matthew it seems has taken some of Jesus' teaching as presented in other settings and placed them here, perhaps to make the realities and values of God's kingdom clear and complete. So in Matthew's collation of this discourse Jesus addresses almost every aspect of their lives; their religious practices and the law, money and real treasure, prayer, relationship with themselves, each other and God.

In His teaching, Jesus develops a bond with them because He is speaking to them about the reality of their lives. He does not alienate nor exclude. But having connected with them, He challenges them, turning upside down their moral code and justice system.

Jesus challenges them to go further, beyond the law, beyond what they know; to love even their enemies, to turn the other cheek, to walk the extra mile. Jesus forms them in the values of God's Kingdom, the values of justice, equality, respect, compassion, forgiveness. He forms them in these Kingdom values by connecting these values to their reality.

Jesus reassures them repeatedly that He knows their reality, their issues and concerns. He teaches them to pray to God as *their* God, the God who would attend to their most basic need of daily bread. He indicates that He knows the things that worry, burden and sadden them. He exhorts them not to worry about things, about clothing, food, money and the things of basic survival. He invites them to trust! How more basic can one get? Jesus taps into the core of their concerns and says that God is with them in it, that God knows all about their needs; so simply trust in God (Mt 6:25–34).

And to give them the courage and incentive to trust in God He tells them that they are more beautiful to God than all the flowers in the field, even more beautiful than Solomon in all his regalia. Jesus lets them know that every hair on their head is known to God, that they are worth more to God than they could ever imagine (6:26–30). Jesus' answer to them about their worries and daily pressures is to set their hearts on God and let tomorrow care for itself. His answer is simply to trust in God (6:33–34).

Somehow the meaning of God's Word reaches the heart of this crowd. Matthew tells us "His teaching made a deep impression on them..." (7:28). How did Jesus manage to make such an impact? By proclaiming the Good News in direct response to their reality. He spoke to them of their lives and their issues. Jesus met them where they were and as they were. He attended to them by reassuring them and affirming them of their importance and worth to God. In this way Jesus made God and God's way accessible and tangible to them.

What is most evident in these examples of Jesus' ministry is His ability to relate with such presence to individuals and even crowds. He had a unique capacity to meet the other's eyes and to touch their heart. He was able to anticipate their hunger and feed them, sense their thirst and refresh them. Jesus could feel their pain and heal them, acknowledge their sin and forgive them. He had the ability to meet them in their brokenness and restore their dignity, to hear their cries and comfort them. Jesus was able to understand their questions, their searching and their longing and fulfil them.

Jesus' ministry brought about miracles and made God real, not through pious religious acts as practised by the Scribes and the Pharisees, but through the stuff of raw human relating. In touch, in gesture, in moments of intimate presence Jesus embodied the God He proclaimed. In Jesus nothing separated God from the immediate and real-life experience of God's people. On the contrary, in Jesus God was fully immersed in the life experience of all those whom He encountered.

For those who were like "mere children", the simple, the lost, the fallen, those whose eyes were not lifted from the earth and whose hearts were not haughty, to such as these the Kingdom of God was revealed. These were the ones who had ears to hear and eyes to see, the ones whose hearts were not hardened. These were the ones who could listen and imagine, the ones for whom the Word produced a rich harvest. These were the ones in whom Jesus' teaching made a deep impression for to them, He taught with a new authority (Mt 7:28).

What was the authority with which Jesus taught? How was His teaching new? What was it about His teaching that left the crowds wanting more, that drove them to seek Him out?

The new authority with which Jesus taught was the *authority of embodiment*. Jesus validated what He taught *about* God by *embodying* the God He proclaimed.

Unlike the Scribes and the Pharisees, Jesus didn't teach about the God of mercy and forgiveness by preaching. He taught about this God by giving them the *experience* of God's mercy and forgiveness. He sat at table with sinners, tax collectors and prostitutes. He associated and allowed Himself to be associated with those whom the religious institution deemed irreligious, and unworthy (Mk 2:15–17). When Jesus taught about the God of love and compassion, He touched lepers, He used His spittle to heal the blind, He embraced children, He went down to those bent over, crippled and twisted and lifted them up.

This was the new authority that impacted upon those who were open to Jesus, the authority of embodiment. In Jesus they did not just hear words *about* God as they did from the Scribes and Pharisees. In Jesus they *saw* God, they *felt* God, they *experienced* God's Presence in a way that they had never experienced it before.

Unlike the teaching of the Scribes and the Pharisees, there were neither contradictions nor discrepancies, no inconsistencies no hypocrisy, no glib or patronizing platitudes in Jesus's teaching. While the Scribes and Pharisees taught about God in dogmas, laws, and heady theology that presented God as being inaccessibly distant to the people, their lives and their sufferings, Jesus' teaching about God was *in direct response to, and in relationship with* the people and their reality. Jesus' teaching brought God into the stuff of their lives, into the nitty gritty reality of their experience.

The model of ministry Jesus left us with is so obvious that we may overlook it for something more theoretical or sophisticated. Essentially it is a model of *authentic relationship*. Practically, Jesus' ministry was about meeting people where they were and as they were, attending to them by allowing Himself to become engaged with them, often just simply in opening Himself to be present to them. Jesus' ministry was essentially about unconditional love.

For Jesus it was love which compelled Him to do what He did in His ministry. Mutual unconditional love is the essence of Jesus' life and ministry. It is the crux of His directive to us to go and do the same (Jn 13:15).

PART TWO: IMPLICATIONS

In this section we want to consider the implications of our scriptural reflection concerning Jesus' ministry. The issues will be addressed here in a broad and general manner and will be discussed in greater detail in the following chapters.

What are the implications of the model of Jesus' ministry for our ministry today? When we step back from our subjective stance and try to assess what is happening in our faith communities we hopefully recognize that there are many good and life-giving experiences within our communities. We will recognise that there are issues and realities to be concerned about and situations that leave much to be desired.

Examining Jesus' ministry enables us to learn from it, to renew and re-focus our ministry in light of what Jesus did. Often the thought of evaluation has negative overtones. We may fear that our limitations and failures will be exposed. Our intention here, as mentioned in our introduction, is to provide the stimulus whereby the strengths and limitations of our ministry can be identified and reviewed in light of Jesus' ministry. With this in mind let us proceed.

1. DISCERNING THE SIGNS OF THE TIMES

An important ingredient in any serious evaluation is the ability to discern the realities of our situation, to read the signs of the times and discern their meaning and implications for us.

a) The comings, goings and absences in our communities

One of the most notable signs for discernment and evaluation within our Church today is the coming and going and absence of people within our communities, in particular within our parish communities. Some would note that people are leaving our communities in droves while others would notice that many new people are joining our communities, especially through the R.C.I.A. program. Does this suggest that some of our communities are struggling and may well be dying, while other communities are growing and flourishing?

Our interest here is not in numbers but in the vitality of the life within our faith communities. What attracts people to join our communities and what keeps them away or even sends them away? Were we to ask those who do not come and those who are leaving the reasons for their choice we may be surprised at what we hear.

We cannot assume that the reason for the empty seats and departures within our communities is because of a lack of faith. Today faith-filled people are leaving us in search of life-giving community, hungry for an experience of God that nourishes their spirit.

Some people are not even bothering to attend our communities, because to attend deadens their spirits or frustrates their hunger or angers their sense of justice. Others are not attending because what they sense and experience is not relevant to their lives and, at worse, is insensitive to their life experience. Some are not meeting God when they come to us so they go or they remain on the edge, filled more with lethargy and apathy than with energy and commitment.

And can we assume that all is well with the faithful ones who come regularly, even through the ups and downs of our communities. What motivates their coming and their staying? How are our communities enriching them and forming them?

What of our absent brethren, in particular the poor and the marginalized within our society, the very remnant that Jesus sought out, where are they in our faith communities today? Is their absence due to their lack of interest, or their struggle for survival, or do they not know where or how to come to us. Do they not experience genuine outreach, or do they sense a lack of welcome and inclusion or even patronizing tolerance?

For those new members who are joining our communities, what is attracting them and drawing them? Is it not that they have experienced some kind of meaningful contact with us, often through a relationship with someone from within our community who has embodied something of God for them, perhaps simply in their friendship or in the witness of their own faith. Those who are joining us are obviously finding the God they seek within our community or they would not come to us.

The comings, the goings, the absences and even the stayings within our communities can tell us so much about the effectiveness of our ministry. We may need to take time to ask our community and those on the edge of our community the reasons for their choices.

b) A crisis of credibility

Impacting upon all of this is a major crisis that is rocking the institutional Church to its core. It is not a crisis about poor Mass attendance, though some would see that as the only issue. It is a crisis of credibility.

In the face of so many cases of abuse, mistrust and deception and in the light of so many contradictions and discrepancies of lifestyle, of leadership and management, some people from within the Church, and those who observe the Church, are sensing, with mixed reactions, a lack of credibility in the Church that some fear may lead to the collapse of the Church as we know it.

More and more people within our communities are questioning not only the Church's teaching, but the Church's values, attitudes and authority. Fewer people are believing and accepting as readily as they did in the past, what is said, done and presented by the Church and its leadership.

There is at grassroots level a radical shifting that has people claim-ing their own voice and their own authority. And their voices are often expressing cries of protest and objection, of concern and frustration. This grassroot swell is calling the Church, particularly its leadership, to accountability, to validate its actions, perhaps even, to validate its very existence.

We could spend much time discussing the crisis which is gripping our Church. We could do well to spend all our time addressing the critical issues of hierarchy and leadership, priesthood and celibacy, the role of women and lay ministry, sexual and emotional abuse, financial and political corruption and injustice and theological and liturgical renewal.

While this list could go on and become very specific, my purpose here is simply to acknowledge that we are truly a broken, human Church. In this sense we are no different from the religious insti-tution that Jesus encountered when He walked this earth.

Just as the people of Jesus' day were disillusioned with their insti-tution, so too, many people today are disillusioned with so much that occurs within our Church. Just as Jesus highlighted the hypocrisy, injustice and lack of mercy and compassion in the reli-gious leadership of His day, so too if He walked our earth today, His challenge to us would be as direct and as uncompromising as it was then.

The point to be made here is that we have in Jesus not only the model for our ministry but we have in Him the way to address the issues and brokenness of our Church. The crisis facing our con-temporary Church may well be a blessing, an opportunity and turning point as the word "crisis" itself suggests, to come back to the heart of the matter, to look to Jesus and His way, to do more faithfully and more genuinely what the Spirit of Jesus empowers us to do.

If we can reclaim through a new vision and a renewed spirit, our real focus as the people of God, then we will see a more authentic body of Christ, a more impassioned and Spirit-filled community.

There are many seeds and blossomings which signify the emergence of a renewed and more Spirit-filled Church. We need to take heart from them. We need to be aware of our human frailty, aware that we each do the best we can, holding in balance our failures as well as our genuine efforts and achievements in honouring the God we proclaim. With this in our hearts and on our minds let us move on to look at some specific areas wherein the model of Jesus' ministry has critical implications for us today.

2. GO AND DO THE SAME

a) Claiming what is of God in us

Jesus ministered out of the depths of His humanity as much as from the glory and power of His divinity. He did not suspend His humanity to do divine things but rather lived from the fullness of His being. This mysterious dialogue in Jesus is the same mystery that we are called to embrace within the depths of our own souls. The ability to do this becomes our best resource for our ministry.

Isn't this ironic, especially in light of the above, that what is most fragile in us, our humanity, is in essence our best resource for ministry. This almost seems absurd in view of our failure and brokenness. But in light of what is possible in our spirits because of Jesus' Spirit, this is awesome. From the fullness of Jesus' life we have received grace upon grace (Jn 1:16). Do we believe it? Do we recognize it?

To go and do the same as Jesus did is first and foremost about claiming the God within us. We need to embrace what is of God in us and minister out of our genuine efforts to live from the empowerment of Jesus' Spirit in us. We need to claim as our greatest gift, who we are before God, using our gifts, talents, skills and the unique expertise of our own personal journey.

To go and do the same as Jesus did is not about being less human, nor about being perfect but about being genuine and real before God. To do as Jesus did is about staying in intimate relationship with the God within, staying close to our God-centre.

Practically this means developing a pattern of prayerful dialogue between the issues of our ministry and the reality of our being; coming to God not just for guidance around the pressures and concerns of our ministry, but coming to God in love for the nurturing for which our spirits long.

Staying close to our God-centre is about deep inner listening and greater self-trust. It's about learning to trust our intuition and inner movement as the seedbed of God's creative wisdom in us. It is about looking inward before we look too hastily outward for resources that could well develop from our own insights and sharing, our own imaginings and creativity. This is the resourcefulness that allows God to work in and through us in ways we never dreamed possible!

b) Having a heart for ministry

To do as Jesus did raises a lot of questions about what motivates and directs our ministry. For Jesus' ministry was about unconditional love, proclaiming in the enfleshment of that love the reign of God. What motivates our ministry today?

One of the significant developments in ministry in the Church today is the wonderful opportunity for training and development. The value of this is that people are qualified and equipped with important and relevant skills, as well as being given the confidence and support they need to fulfil their responsibilities.

A potential danger here, however, is that ministry may become more about *career* and less about doing what Jesus did. It is a fine line that distinguishes ministry from career. The line is drawn not by qualifications but by *motivation*. This is a delicate issue since we cannot judge the motivation of an individual's heart. It is the fruits that are borne which very often reveal what is in the heart. There are, I believe, signs in some areas of our Church that suggest a career mentality has taken hold, bringing with it the paper-chase mentality, as though having the qualification gives one the heart for ministry.

We need to clarify our stance here. Gaining qualifications is an important and necessary requirement for ministry today for many reasons. Apart from the direct benefits to ministry it does, in some cases, lead to more just and fair wages. Many dedicated people have ministered and still minister in our communities without receiving adequate pay. Some, especially those with families, have to make considerable sacrifices in order to meet their basic needs. This is, as we all know, far from the ideal. If gaining qualifications and expertise brings with it better wages then well and good, although one questions if just and fair wages should depend solely on qualifications.

This is not our concern here. Our real concern is when the qualification is seen and used to be the measure of someone's suitability for ministry. What about the heart for ministry? What about personal integrity, vitality of faith and the credibility of one's experience? Are we giving these due consideration? What is the ultimate measure of a person's qualification in ministry—a piece of paper or the integrity of their being? When the paper-chase is motivated by politics and ambition and when it overrides the heart for ministry then, I believe, we have real problems.

We need to keep coming back to Jesus. It was unconditional love that motivated His ministry and through that love He established the reign of God. This is not to suggest in any way that love is all that is needed for ministry! There is no question here about the need for training and qualification. The question and concern is around a loss of balance and perspective; a loss of the necessary heart for ministry.

Motivation for ministry that stems from ego or power or ambition tends to breed a certain corrosive atmosphere and attitude in ministry that is often driven by efficiency and performance. Ministry in such cases tends to become more administrative and less relational, more task-orientated and less person-centred. We can experience in such environments, politicising, ambition, defensiveness, a lack of mutuality, injustice and a loss of heart.

We know situations such as this. We know the frustration and pain that can cripple people's spirits within such situations. So easily we lose sight of the person and the heart of the matter. We become so introspective and caught up in our power and empire building that we fail to recognize the human face of God and can, at worse, contradict by our values, attitudes and policies the very nature of the God we are proclaiming.

We know within our very human Church, organizations and situations wherein even the basic values of respect, mutuality, kindness, understanding and charity are denied workers and/or members. Services may be efficient and plentiful here but the heart is in pain and, somehow in the system, it is uncared for and at times unjustly treated.

Balancing this reality are the many organizations and communities that truly give life to those who are involved in them. By their warmth, hospitality, openness, respect, pastoral concern and the vitality of the spirit of their people, God is known, and the values of God's Kingdom are evident.

If doing what Jesus did in ministry is essentially about love that liberates and gives life then we need to look very seriously at what motivates and directs our ministry and the ministry of our organizations and institutions. We will know by the quality of relationships what is at the heart of our ministry and our organizations.

Ministry requires a special kind of heart, a "heart of flesh", the same heart that Jesus embodied. And those who need to experience that heart of flesh in us are not just those to whom we minister, but in a special way our own colleagues and co-workers. In many ways it is harder to do it for our own than it is to do it for strangers!

3. EMBODYING THE GOD WE PROCLAIM

a) Providing opportunities for people to experience God

Jesus' ministry challenges us to examine not only the *why* of our ministry, the heart and motivation of it, but the *how* of our ministry today. In reflecting upon how Jesus proclaimed God's reign, we saw that He validated all that He proclaimed about God by giving the experience of that God. We are called to do the same, to provide opportunities in our communities for our people to experience God.

This may seem obvious, since isn't that what we are concerned with in our ministry? It may be our objective but is it our reality?

Karl Rahner in addressing what is at the heart of our spirituality said that "the most basic phenomenon of Christian spirituality is the experience of God as Presence, intimate, relatable Presence." (1) The most perfect embodiment of that Presence is Jesus. We see in Jesus' ministry that the God of Jesus is not a theory or notion or theological doctrine to be *taught*, but is Presence to be *experienced*, a living dynamic being who lavishes love and grace upon us, calling forth life in us.

The God of Jesus is a relational God who is ever-present to us, ever-loving and yet, paradoxically, incomprehensible mystery to us. The extraordinary reality of this God is that even beyond our lack of a consciously-felt sense of God in our lives, God is constantly gracing our humanity. (2)

This is the God who sent the prophet Jeremiah down to the potter's house so that, in beholding what the potter does to the clay, Jeremiah would understand what it is like to be in relationship with this God (Jer 18:1–6). This is the God who in giving us Jesus went well beyond images, even beyond the cross, to declare the nature and intention of God's relationship with us.

Experiencing God is not exclusive to mystical experience. God is present in *all* human experience. In this sense the experience of God is both immanent and transcendent. Jesus' life and ministry attests to this in a most radical and profound way. In Jesus the experience of God was, as Rahner says, "bursting out of the very heart of human existence." (3)

It was Jesus who made God real and present in human existence. It is none other than ourselves, by virtue of Jesus' Spirit within us, who are called to be the human embodiment of God's Presence for those whom we encounter. We are called to provide in who we are and in what we do, opportunities wherein God is real and accessible in the lives of those to whom we minister.

This is an awesome privilege and responsibility. It is only possible because in God nothing is impossible! It is possible in as much as grace empowers us to claim the God within us.

It is easier to theorize about this mystery than it is to live it. In real terms we need to grapple with and own the truths of what we proclaim and teach about God, first within our own being, not in a once-and-for-all sense, but in a momentary, everyday sense of coming to terms with mystery. In the reality of this constant challenge and struggle in our own lives, and through the grace that both empowers it and issues from it, we embody in the way we relate to others, the God of Jesus.

We provide opportunities for people to experience the God of Jesus when we enter into life-giving relationship with them, when we are genuinely present to them, when in our relating and manner of being with them, we make real and accessible the experience of God's love and mercy, God's compassion and justice, God's intimate Presence.

Rahner believes that without the experience of God as personal relatable Presence, all our theology, all our teaching and doctrines, our worship and rituals are irrelevant and without meaning, are dull and deadened.(4) It is fundamentally the experience of God's Presence that makes sense of and validates all that we proclaim and do in our ministry.

Could this be the issue determining the comings and goings, the absences and the stayings within our communities? Are we failing, in some situations, in our relationships, our practices and our worship to provide opportunities wherein God's Presence is known and experienced? This is the most legitimate measure of our effectiveness in ministry, that in who we are and in what we do God is known.

What are the indicators of God's Presence in our community? How is God experienced as personal, relatable Presence within our community life, especially within our liturgy and worship?

We may need to talk to our people in order to assess this realistically. We may need to discern the signs: the energy level and vitality of our community gatherings, the spirit of participation and reverence in our liturgies. We know the Sacred is in our midst when we sense we are on holy ground. When and where is our communal ground holy? What makes it holy ground?

The evidence of God's Presence in our midst is not in emotional euphoria or gushy sentiment, nor is it necessarily in high solemnity and intense fervour. The evidence is as it was in Jesus, embodied in people's spirits, in the basic virtues of goodness, compassion, respect, justice and good old-fashioned kindness.

Love is the sign by which we are known as Jesus' disciples (Jn 13:34–35). It is as basic as that! What then is the measure of love in our communities? What are our relationships like? Are our people being nourished on their journey? Are they being challenged, formed and affirmed? Is there genuine joy and a sense of wellbeing in their coming together? Are the values of God's Kingdom evident in the life and activities of our community? These are some of the indicators of the Presence of God. The ones that matter most are the ones that are identified in your community.

b) Meeting people where they are

If our ministry is to be life-giving then, in a deliberate and intentional manner, we need to take up some of the principles modelled in Jesus' ministry. In our faith education, in our liturgy and worship, in our welfare services and outreach programs, in whatever area we minister, we need to meet people where they are and as they are within their life-experience.

With a spirit of genuine interest and concern, we need to find a way to connect with our people on *their* ground and come to know something of their story. Too often in ministry, and almost exclusively in some ministries, people are expected to come to us on our terms, into the territory of our values, attitudes, practices and life experience, regardless of their ease, or comfort or readiness.

Jesus showed us how to connect with people in a spirit of mutuality and equality wherein real needs can be met and life-giving relationships can be formed. The problem here for most of us is that we are often in crisis-mode or survival-mode. We are so pressured in our efforts to simply do the bare essentials that we do not have time to connect with individuals and families. They may be familiar to us and we may have some sense of their presenting circumstances and needs but we don't know the real stuff of their lives.

We are not advocating here imposed disclosure or invasion of privacy or intrusive interaction or programs and activities that create artificial relationships. We are, however, stressing the need for the kind of sensitivity, intuition, interest and concern that typified Jesus' ministry, that promotes warmth and approachability in our contact with those to whom we minister.

It is not just that we don't know the story or circumstances of our people that is important here. It is that we may not have integrated into our structures and initiatives opportunity for them and ourselves to connect with their daily reality. It is as though we expect, when people come to our communities, that they get on with the purpose at hand despite where and what they come from!

This is evident, for example, in some of our schools where we don't know what some of our students have to live through before they come to us, or what they have to return to when they leave us. The pressures, anxieties, heartaches and abuse that some of our children live with is well beyond what we as adults could or would endure. Yet we expect them to come and be fully present and fully functional in our classes, to attend to the things that we insist are important to them and their lives.

Do we take time to connect with them and sense how they are? Do we pick up the vibes and discern the reasons for the presenting behaviour of our children, or do we simply get on with it, disciplining at times insensitively and ineffectively, completely unaware or disinterested in what is happening in their hearts?

Do we give our children time and opportunity to connect with themselves, with each other and with their God, before we allow our systems, routines and demands to devour them? Do we meet our children where they are and as they are? Do we provide opportunities for them to experience God as real and present in the circumstances of their lives?

And what of those within our parishes, who come to our liturgy and worship? Do we know anything about the stuff of their daily lives? Do we have a finger on the pulse of our community, on the energy, concerns, pressures and heartaches that dictate their lives? If not, how can we provide meaningful liturgy? How can we break open the Word in the reality of their life experience if we are uninvolved with and disconnected from them?

To meet our people where they are will demand of us a spirit willing to befriend; a sensitive and intuitive spirit. It will see us integrating into our community, structures, programs, worship and rituals, that give our people the opportunity to be together, providing them with the atmosphere which enables them to feel welcome, comfortable and at home with us and with the wider community.

Meeting people where they are is not about being social welfare workers or intrusive gossipers! It is about being present, as Jesus was, through the basic human qualities of warmth and sensitivity, respect and acceptance. It is often in the little things, in the simplest expressions of human relating that we are able to connect with those to whom we minister.

Meeting people where they are is also about a willingness in us to move out from our territory into the territory of the real life of our people, to meet them on their ground. It is about taking the Good News from our Churches into the homes, neighbourhoods and sometimes squalour of people's lives. It is about being open to finding God in the most unlikely places and situations, to be present and perhaps more real than the enclosures and complacency of our structures and institutions usually allow God to be. No-one has done that more effectively than Jesus!

c) Attending to People and their needs

Jesus' ministry challenges us to do more than provide programs and services in meeting the needs of our communities. Jesus attended to needs and at the same time *met the heart* of those He tended. This is often where we fall short. Jesus shows us that ministry is more about relationship than about fixing problems, more about being with than about doing, more about meeting hearts than about running programs.

We are very good at the practical and administrative aspects of our ministry, solving problems, giving advice and running programs. We are not as good at being present to another, being sensitive and intuitive to the real needs. Is our ministry about meeting needs or is it about meeting people and attending to them? That is the difference between service and ministry. That is the difference between Jesus' way and our way. We may well be providing excellent services to people in our community and that may be all some of our community desire from us. But are we connecting with people and in the connection are we ministering to them and their needs from the God-centre within us?

Again one of the biggest difficulties here is that often the pressures we have in our ministry and a real lack of time prevent us from responding as we would truly want to respond. And so children for example slip through our schools unnoticed and unknown to us.

Individuals and families drift in and out of our worship without being noticed or connecting. Have they experienced God in and through their contact with us? We may never know. The consolation for us is that we know that the revelation and experience of God is not dependent on us. In spite of us and our limitations, God breaks into people's lives in ways we could never imagine. Nevertheless, we may need to prioritize our activities and services more in keeping with the values of God's Kingdom. This may ease some of the excessive pressure and frantic pace that so many of us experience in our ministry.

There is no doubt that people are overloaded and stressed, particularly in our school communities. The absurd amount of paper work, the constant pressure of appraisals and inspections and upgrading, drain the energy and spirit of our teachers, limiting their capacity to do what matters most in their ministry in Catholic schools.

When people are stressed and demoralised they cannot give their best. How can we slow down, simplify and ease up in our ministry so that we notice what really matters?

This challenge is so important. We know that we need to provide practical support as well as pastoral support. How do we find the balance? In providing good efficient administration and services, we need to be aware of whom we are serving, not lose sight of individuals and their realities, nor harden our own hearts or overshadow our presence with frantic activity, while all the time the cry and the longing of another is unheeded by us.

We need to remember that it was in the stuff of human relating that Jesus attended to the needs of those He encountered, even when He had to face the organizational nightmare of feeding five thousand with just five loaves and two fish! We will probably never have the energy or breadth of love to attend to all who cross our path. Without wanting to be too idealistic and unreal the point here is that somehow we need to find the balance between being task-orientated and being person-centred.

In the hectic pace of our daily lives finding the balance is as basic as noticing how we welcome people, how we greet them, how we respond to them and reach out to them, how we listen to and hear them. The reality is that a simple smile, word or gesture can turn it all around!

d) Teaching with a new authority

i) In response to and in relationship with life experience.

We have already discussed how Jesus taught with a new authority which made a deep impression upon those who were open to Him. What kind of impression does our teaching make? Do we leave our children, youth and adults wanting more of the God we proclaim?

When we teach and proclaim God do we do it the way Jesus did, in response to and in relationship with our people and their life experience? Or do we bring our people in, sit them down and "hit" them with the gospel of Jesus, time after time, as though it were a garment that we cloak ourselves in or a whitewash that soothes over all other realities! And we wonder why many of our people experience our teaching to be irrelevant. We wonder why they are unmoved, unchallenged and uninspired.

We have noted several times that Jesus proclaimed the Word of God and the Good News of God's Kingdom in the context of people's real life. We need to be aware of and in dialogue with the lives of our people, just as Jesus was with the crowds He taught. If our teaching is going to make a deep impression it will be because we have connected in some way with the hearts and lives of those we are addressing.

ii) Validating our teaching by embodiment.

Do we teach and proclaim God as the Pharisees did or do we do what Jesus did? Do we validate our teaching and proclamation of God by providing opportunities for our people to come into the experience of the God we proclaim?.

Is what we declare about God in our community, authenticated and validated by what people experience of God in our presence and in the life of our community? Are people experiencing in us the face of the God of Jesus whom we proclaim, the heart and mind of that God and the values and attitudes of that God? Do we resemble the image and likeness of the God we are proclaiming?

Or are we contradicting the God we proclaim? Are we creating discrepancies and inconsistencies which present God as being at odds with our reality, aloof, distant and inaccessible? How do our structures, policies, values, affirmations, admonitions and expectations validate or contradict the nature of the God of Jesus?

The credibility and authority of our teaching today is measured in very practical ways and in very subtle ways. Diocesan and parochial policies, for example, of acceptability and admission into our communities can create serious discrepancies about the God we proclaim and the God we embody in practice.

What are we saying about God when we refuse admission to and acceptance in our communities to individuals on the basis of selective criteria which we deem to be a worthy measure of an individual's suitability? What are we saying to and about those we exclude, for example, because they do not attend our worship every Sunday, or they can't contribute x amount of money or their marital status is not the norm? Are we not saying to them, what the Pharisees said to the outcast, whom Jesus not only welcomed, but with whom He associated?

In the light of the values of God's Kingdom, we cannot justify such policies of admission or exclusion as being legitimate because we are under financial pressure or our numbers are too big or our resources are too limited. The challenge here is to develop more creative ways to address those very real problems without acting in a manner contrary to the God with whom we claim to be involved.

A good measure here is to look at our communities to see if they resemble in any way the crowds who followed Jesus. Do we have in our communities the people whom Jesus would welcome to His table? Or are we including in our communities only those who measure up to be "practising their faith" according to our criteria which, if we are not careful, might be more recognizable as the Pharisees' criteria than as Jesus' criteria for identifying who God's people really are (Mt 9:10–13).

If we proclaim a God of love and compassion, equality and mutuality, mercy and justice then that God must be made flesh in all aspects of our community. We must, if our faith is to be credible, develop and uphold policies and values, structures and initiatives that honour and reflect the God we proclaim. It is as basic as being aware of whom and what we affirm or fail to affirm, whom or what we promote or stand up against, whom or what we welcome and deem acceptable.

The measure of what we do and don't do must be Jesus. We need to focus our awareness on what Jesus did and what He would do in our situation. We need to keep asking ourselves and each other how authentic we are? We need to ask ourselves and each other are we aware of and in touch with the bigger picture of people's lives and their reality? Do we understand, can we empathize, are we compassionate, are we trying to be fair and just, forgiving and reconciling? Are we able to welcome and accept those whom Jesus would welcome and accept? Are we able to meet the eyes of our people, touch their hearts and be present to them?

These questions are not about how perfect we are, but how human we are. They are questions about how well we are relating to people. And this is how basic ministry in the model of Jesus' ministry really is.

We will proceed, after our personal discernment, to focus on some specific aspects of Jesus' ministry and consider in greater detail their implications for our ministry today.

PART THREE: RESPONDING TO THE IMPLICATIONS

Personal Synthesis:

1. What feelings do these reflections stir in you?

2. What issues and concerns do they raise for you?

3. What insights would you like to add to these reflections?

4. Who are the individuals in your life who have embodied God for you? What have they taught you about God? How have they done this?

5. What is it of God that you need to claim more deeply in your own life? How could this enrich your ministry?

   In what special way do you embody God for those to whom you minister?

6. What is one thing you proclaim about God that you grapple with in your own life? Can you share this with someone who may understand your struggle?

Scripture reflection:

Take some quiet time to reflect on one of the following text.

The Woman at the Well (Jn 4:1–30)

The Widow of Nain (Lk 7:11–17)

The Beatitudes (Mt 5:3–12)

• Quieten your spirit and visualize yourself in the encounter. Imagine that you are the person to whom Jesus attends. Where would He meet you? How would He find your spirit? How would He attend to you? What does He reveal to you of yourself? What does He reveal to you of God?

Hold that revelation quietly within you.

For group sharing:

• Allow the group time to connect and gather before you begin discussing these questions. It is important to be aware of people's energy and readiness for what is to follow. In light of this, it may be more appropriate to be selective with these questions or even to disregard them and find another way for your group to respond to the implications.

1.   Share in some way with the group something of your own personal synthesis of these reflections.

2.   What questions, concerns and issues do these reflections raise for you as a ministry team within your community?

3.   What are the signs for discernment and evaluation in your community? What is one thing you can initiate that might enable the discernment to begin?

4.   What are the seeds and blossomings of renewal in your community? How can you nurture, sustain and develop them? How can you celebrate them?

5.   In what way do you embody in your ministry, the God you proclaim? What are the values, policies, practices and initiatives within your community that honour the God of Jesus and which are those that may contradict the nature of the God you proclaim?

6.   What initiatives do you have that enable your community to know each other better? How can you as a team be more aware of the realities of your community? How can you take the Good News out into your neighbourhood?

7.   What impact is your teaching and proclamation of God, having on your community, especially in your liturgy and faith education? What factors are contributing to this?

8.   How well do you as a team hold the balance between task and people? What are some of the administrative and struc-

tural pressures that force you into crisis and survival mode? What can be done about these pressures? How can you be more nurturing of yourself and each other in your ministering?

9. Plan a time and a process to enable you to work on a team statement on what motivates and directs your ministry within your community.

RITUAL AND PRAYER

• The following are suggestions that may assist you in bringing your sharing to prayer. They are only suggestions and should not be considered in any other way. It would be better to create your own prayer and ritual than to rely on something that comes from outside your sharing.

Suggestions:

1. Create a sacred space and atmosphere of quiet and stillness within the group. Soften lights if necessary and play some quiet background music. Light a candle and place the Word and or relevant symbols within the centre of the group. Try to integrate into the sacred space something that has come from your sharing. Ensure that people are able to see the sacred focus, that they are comfortable and ready to enter into the prayerful spirit of this time.

2. Plan before the meeting a process that could be integrated into your prayer, that would enable each of your team members to comfortably and reverently share in the following:

   Consider a quality of God that each member of your team embodies. Consider how you see them integrating this quality of God in their ministry. Find an appropriate way to ritualize this affirmation with each member of your team.

3. The following scripture may be appropriate:
   1 Cor 3:16–17

1 Cor 12:4–11
2 Cor 4:7–10
Jn 15:9–17

4. Some of the following songs may be helpful (please refer to page 191 for location of songs):
    Gather Us O God (ARH)
    Song of God's People (ARH)
    All Praise Glory And Honour (ARH)
    God Is...(GI)
    This Is Your Way (COJ)
    Lead Me Guide Me (BUH)
    To The Glory Of God (BUH)

5. At the conclusion of your prayer share a meal or a drink or something that will enable people to celebrate and or de-brief.

CHAPTER 3

WARMTH, AFFECTION, INTIMACY

PART ONE: SCRIPTURAL REFLECTION

When we reflect in the gospels on Jesus' miracles and His encounters with people, it is evident to the heart that can see, that God's compassionate, healing and merciful Presence were enfleshed and manifest in the seemingly natural warmth and affection of Jesus.

Gospel texts will often note that Jesus touched or embraced or laid His hands upon someone in need, or that He looked with love, or was moved with pity or felt someone's pain. Such passing comments reveal much about the person of Jesus.

In this chapter we want to give special attention to the affective quality of Jesus' ministry, reflecting on the warmth and intimacy of

His Presence and the issues this raises for us personally and for our ministry.

Let us clarify what we are meaning here when we refer to Jesus as a warm and affectionate person. This is more easily clarified by saying that we are not talking about gushy emotionalism, the kind of warm fuzzy huggy mentality that crept into our society and Church in the late seventies and early eighties.

To say that Jesus touched others and allowed Himself to be touched by them, means far more in this context than physicality. It suggests rather, that Jesus had the capacity to come into contact with another, to move another's spirit deeply. It means that Jesus was able to sense feeling and to provoke feeling not just with the touch of His hands but in and through His whole being. Jesus was in this sense a deeply intimate person who bore His intimacy with integrity.

Intimacy is an ambiguous word in our society today. More often than not it is used to imply nothing more than physical and sexual interaction. In our context here when we use the word intimate we are implying its deepest and truest meaning.

Intimacy is a discovery, a revelation, an experience of what is innermost in one's own being and the being of another. It is the capacity to come into the depth or heart of the other to uncover inner deep reality and truth. Intimacy implies a disclosure and a knowing of what is outwardly inaccessible or unseen. (1) Intimacy senses and recognizes in another, or in an experience, that there is more than what meets the eye.

As with all aspects of our human nature, Jesus embodied the best and most authentic expression of intimacy. The gospels reveal a deep sensitivity in His being, a vulnerability and tenderness that allowed Him the ease to be both responsive and receptive in the face of human emotion and experiences.

Jesus' warmth and affection sprang from the depths of His intimate spirit. He could sympathize and empathize with those who suffered. Jesus could express His own heartache, allowing Himself to weep, for example, at the death of His friend, Lazarus (Jn 11:35). And, as we saw in our earlier reflections on the anointing of Jesus' feet by Mary, Lazarus' sister, Jesus allowed Himself to be nurtured and receive affection from others (Jn 12:1–11).

Apart from His attempt at times to avoid the crowds, Jesus didn't protect Himself from the mingling crowds, which at times pressed so closely around Him they were stifling Him (Lk 8:42). Jesus got out there with the people. He visited them and accepted hospitality from them. He became involved in people's lives and developed mutually loving friendships.

The warmth and intimacy of Jesus and its impact upon His ministry and proclamation of God, can be better appreciated here by reflecting upon some of Jesus' miracles and encounters.

Our first example is a most interesting encounter between Jesus and a deaf man (Mk7:31–37). This encounter is interesting, not just in the way Jesus heals the deaf man, but in the many questions it raises for us who were not present.

The text has Jesus surrounded by a crowd. "They" present to Him a deaf man who also had a speech impediment (7:32). There is no indication in the text as to who "they" are. This leaves many of the subsequent events in the story open to interesting interpretation, which can throw fascinating light on the whole experience of this encounter. Let us consider some of these questions.

Who are "they" who present the deaf man to Jesus? Are we left to presume that "they" are the deaf man's family or friends; those who love him and want healing for him? Or are "they" people in the crowd who are anxious to see Jesus "do His thing"; perhaps the cynics, the critics wanting to catch Jesus out? Or could "they" be the Scribes or the Pharisees; those watching and waiting, as they so often did, for Jesus to say or do anything which they could use against Him (Mk 3:1–3)?

And why does the deaf man need to be presented to Jesus? Why doesn't he just present himself? Did he not know, because of his disabilities, how to explain himself to Jesus or did he not know who Jesus was? Had he not experienced Jesus' Presence as many others had? Did he not know what was going on? Why didn't he just burst through the crowd and touch Jesus as others had done in other encounters (Lk 8:40–56)? Or was the deaf man disillusioned with miracle workers; was he sceptical and cynical himself? Or perhaps the deaf man was too afraid, too timid and hesitant to approach Jesus.

There are so many perspectives to this encounter and each of them can shed light on why Jesus does what he does with this man in taking him away from the crowd. In other miracle encounters Jesus heals in the thick of the crowd, even at times because of the faith of the crowd (Mk 2:6). But in this case Jesus takes the one in need away from the crowd where, as Mark says, Jesus could be alone with him (7:33). Why?

Did Jesus take the man away from the crowd because he was sensitive enough to this deaf man to know that when Jesus had restored the man's hearing, the man might be overwhelmed by the crowd's noise and energy? Or did Jesus take the man away from the crowd because Jesus sensed the disbelief or the cynicism in the crowd and refused to entertain them? Or did Jesus Himself need to be alone with this man in order to be fully present and focused on him and his needs; in order to give this man everything Jesus had?

Such questions are more than interesting. They are important in that they can reveal so much about the person of Jesus and the way He relates. And how does He relate to this man? There, alone with this man, Jesus "puts his fingers in the man's ears and His spittle on the man's tongue and then looking up to heaven He sighed and said to the deaf man, 'Ephphatha', that is 'Be open'. And the deaf man's ears were opened and the ligament of his tongue was loosened and he could speak clearly." (7:33–35).

Jesus related to this man with His whole being, Presence, touch, spittle and sighs! He had gathered up all of Himself and had given it as healing power to this man.

In this intimate encounter Jesus revealed the grace at work in His sensitivity, in His full and total Presence to the man and in His touch. But there's more. There is spittle! What is its significance in this encounter?

To appreciate the significance of this, we need to first understand what spittle is. It is literally the juice of life, without it we are dead. And how did Jesus' spittle get on the man's tongue? Did He place it on the man's tongue with His hand or fingers or did He kiss the man in some way? We could speculate for many hours on that question and on many other questions raised in this encounter. The measure of the validity and credibility of such questions is how much our answers are in keeping with the character of Jesus, that is, in keeping with the authenticity and integrity of Jesus's whole life and mission.

The fact is we do not know how Jesus passes His spittle onto the man's tongue. Nor is how He does it nearly as important as the fact that Jesus heals this man with the very juice of His own life! This reveals something far more than the extent of Jesus' warmth and affection, and His capacity for intimacy. It exposes the raw and utterly real breadth and depth of Jesus' humanity and how in and through that miracles happen.

In Jesus' Presence, in His hands, in His spittle and in the powerful breath of His word, "Ephphatha", healing was given to this man.

What would have been the deaf man's first word to Jesus? Whatever it was and whatever he said about Jesus fired the crowds with even more admiration for Jesus. My sense is that, in a special way as a result of how Jesus healed this man, there would have been much talk about how strikingly real and intimate Jesus was. And that is the point to be made here. Jesus ministered so effectively out of His natural warmth and affection. Only one who is fully at home with one's self and fully centred in God could risk such intimacy and bring about such healing!

Jesus didn't always initiate the touch of those He encountered. Our next reflection shows how Jesus allowed Himself to be touched and in doing so, a remarkable healing occurs and through it, God's power is revealed. It is the story of the woman with a haemorrhage. It is Mark (5:21–34) and Luke's (Lk 8:40–56) account of this story that we will use for our reflection since there is some consistency there, as well as far more detail than in Matthew's account (Mt 9:18–26).

Again, Jesus is surrounded by a large crowd, seemingly without any specific purpose other than allowing them to welcome Him back from the country of Gerasenes. Into the crowd comes Jairus, a synagogue official, who pleads with Jesus to come to his house and heal his little daughter who is dying. Jesus responds to Jairus' cry for help and as He journeys to Jairus' home the crowd presses in around Jesus so intensely that Luke reports, "they were stifling Him" (8:42).

No doubt the crowd would have picked up the sudden sense of direction and immediate purpose in Jesus as He made His way to Jairus' home. In view of Jairus' request, many would be wondering how Jesus would deal with the situation, hoping and expecting to witness a miracle, keen to stay close to Jesus so as not to miss anything that He might say or do. No doubt the crowd assumes an intense energy of expectation, urgency and excitement.

And Jesus is in the thick of it. So too is a woman, a special woman. She has been suffering from a haemorrhage for twelve years and Mark says, despite her efforts to be cured, she had not been able to find anyone or anything to relieve her (5:26). Apart from the religious implications of a harsh and stringent law that burdened women in menstruation with rituals of washing and isolation (Lv 15:19–30), this woman was also burdened all those years, as any woman could appreciate, with the physical, emotional, psychological and no doubt, social dis-ease and suffering that is associated with such a condition. We can, in view of this, assume that this woman was desperate!

What had been her intention in being part of this crowd surrounding Jesus? Was she planning to approach Jesus in some way at the right time or was she still trying to sort out her options or her position? Perhaps it was the thought that she may not get the chance to do anything once Jesus reached Jairus' house that forced the woman to act immediately in any way she could. Mark tells us the woman thought if she could touch even just the fringe of Jesus' garment she felt there would be a chance to be well again (5:28). Another indication perhaps of how desperate this woman was!

Where was the woman situated in the crowd in relation to Jesus? Was she near Him or did she have to fight her way through the crowd in order to reach out and touch Him? From wherever she was situated and with whatever physical and emotional energy it took, the woman reached out, through this thronging crowd and touched the back of Jesus' cloak. Instantly the bleeding stopped! Immediately Jesus turned round and asked "Who touched me?"

Given the stifling crowd, this was to the disciples an absurd question, especially given their struggle of trying to protect Jesus, while keeping the crowd in order. But regardless of their efforts to convince Jesus that, given the crowd, everyone was touching Him, Jesus remains firm, insisting that this was not just any touch; someone had touched right through the crowd and its hustle and bustle into the very core of Jesus and Jesus knew it because He had felt it!

Jesus looked all around the crowd to see who had touched Him. How did Jesus identify the one who had touched Him in such a way that He felt power had gone out from Him (Lk 8:46). And what was the woman feeling as He stopped and asked His question? Probably, while trying to come to terms with what had just happened for her physically, the woman was now having to deal with being exposed; fearing the many consequences and shame of being in a public situation while being legally impure (Lv 15:25), as well as her uncertainty about how Jesus might respond to her.

But somehow, according to Luke she "sees" herself to be discovered (8:47). How? Was Jesus' look so intense that it penetrated beyond the crowd into her very soul? Somehow the woman experiences herself to be discovered, exposed and in full view of the One who had just relieved her in her most desperate need. How did she feel? She comes out trembling and falls at Jesus' feet. Imagine the stillness and the silence in the crowd as she tells her story. Having brought about by the power of His Presence, a remarkable healing for this woman, Jesus attends now to her spirit. He not only restores her in her health but affirms her and restores her dignity (8:48). Now the healing is complete.

Again, there are many questions that arise from this encounter. What was the power that Jesus felt had left Him when the woman touched Him? How did He experience it as leaving Him? In the face of such an extraordinary mystery I am not qualified to even attempt to answer such questions. All I know is that unlike the less than human Superman character, Jesus must have been incredibly present and self-aware to know so surely that something had happened in Him; that He in fact had been deeply touched.

This encounter is a very beautiful reflection of Jesus' self-intimacy; His extraordinary ability to be so in tune with His being that He could experience under such circumstances the touch of one so desperate. The healing in this encounter occurs through the power of Jesus' Presence that is so sacred, so intimate it not only penetrates, in some way, the woman's body, bringing forth physical healing, but penetrates to her very soul bringing forth the healing of her spirit.

Had Jesus not sought this woman out from within the crowd her healing might not have been so complete. In acknowledging that He had been touched, Jesus enabled the woman to come forth from the darkness of her hidden, shameful state, into the light of His affirmation and restoration of her dignity. This happens, it seems, when one can overcome the fear and trembling that keeps one hidden and lost in shame and enables one to be discovered by Jesus.

There are many other examples of how Jesus ministered through His sensitive, intimate Presence or through His healing touch. Jesus' healing of the leper for example (Mk 1:40–45), is not just about making one who is "unclean" clean, but it is about *how* the leper is cleansed and *how* his dignity is restored. When we appreciate that lepers were never touched by those who were "clean", we then begin to appreciate that what Jesus does for the leper is so extraordinary. Jesus did not step back from the leper and extend a blessing! Jesus came right into the heart of the leper's disease and suffering and touched it so deeply with His hands that the disease was healed.

Jesus connects with human disease and mess in the warmth of His touch. And in that touch, when nothing separates human suffering and mess from the touch of Jesus, miracles happen.

Jesus' touch was not always physical. With the rich young man in Mark's gospel we see that Jesus' touch can be through a penetrating look (Mk 10:17–22). How did it come to be reported that "Jesus looked steadily at him and loved him" (10:21)? What did the rich young man or those who witnessed this communicate to others about the experience?

Somehow the look that Jesus gave this young man must have been so special that there was no doubt in either the young man's heart or in the awareness of others, that he was loved by Jesus. What was in the eyes of Jesus as He looked at this young man? Perhaps it was the fullness and perfection of what is in the eyes of any loving parent who looks upon their child, or what is in the eyes of any friend or lover who beholds their beloved?

When Jesus looked steadily at this young man, He looked upon all of us in our limitations, our lack of readiness and our inability to let go, lovingly understanding and accepting us in our humanity. And the steady look of Jesus that the young man knew to be a look of love remains imprinted upon our hearts, as no doubt it remained imprinted on the young man's heart, not only reminding us of the constant love of our God but luring us and inviting us to eventually let go and surrender to that love.

We will let one of our mystics, Nicholas of Cusa have the last word on this.

My experience proves that you love me because your eyes are so attentively upon me...Lord your glance is love. And just as your gaze beholds me so attentively that it never turns from me, even so it is with your love. (2)

PART TWO: IMPLICATIONS

The close attention here to Jesus' warmth, affection and intimacy and its effectiveness in the embodiment of God's loving, healing Presence, invites us to address the issues concerning our own presence in ministry.

There are delicate issues to be addressed here because this area of affectivity and intimacy is deeply personal and is dealt with and expressed differently by each of us. Some struggle to find ease in this, while others struggle because of the ease and spontaneity of their warmth and affection. The delicacy of this matter is not just around our own personal agenda, but in an even more urgent way, it is concerned with the sexual abuse crisis within our Church.

Those who suffer as victims of abuse; those who have been abused and those who have abused are the ones who are most qualified to address the issues involved. The most we can hope to do here is to acknowledge the seriousness of the problem and some of its consequences upon our ministry, while being sensitively aware of the suffering that it has brought to so many in our community.

I would propose that underpinning both our personal agenda concerning affectivity in ministry, as well as the issues rising from the abuse crisis in our Church, there is a deeper crisis, a crisis of intimacy, in particular, a real struggle in the area of self-intimacy. The issues related to this are far reaching, not just in terms of our own personal journey but also for our ministry.

Therefore, before we look at the specific implications of Jesus' model in this area of ministry, let us first consider the crisis at hand.

1. INTIMACY AND SELF-INTIMACY

As mentioned earlier the sense of intimacy implied here is beautifully manifested in Jesus' exceptional ability to touch into the very core of another's soul simply by His Presence. Given that intimacy is about one's capacity to experience inner truth and meaning, to appreciate mystery and sacredness, then it is no surprise that one's capacity for intimacy is dependent on one's ability to be self-intimate.

Self-intimacy is about one's ability to see and know the depths of one's own being. It is the ability to live *with* one's self, not in the sense of self-absorption or isolation, but in the sense of knowing one's truth, owning one's brokenness, embracing one's fears and all that prevents one from coming home to one's self in a spirit of wellbeing and acceptance.

The ability to *befriend* one's self is a true mark of self-intimacy. To *be* friend to one's self is about listening to one's inner journey, attending to it and growing in loving appreciation of the intricacies and qualities that give shape to one's being. It is about the kind of self-love and self-respect that enables one to hold in balance the strengths and weakness of one's being, allowing self-forgiveness and self-compassion to be healing grace in one's journey towards claiming one's truest and most authentic being.

Implicit in this understanding of self-intimacy is the realization that at the heart of our deepest and truest self is the God of indwelling. We see here that self-intimacy is intrinsically engaged with God as the One who knows my being beyond all knowing. Thomas Merton says that "the depths of my identity is in the centre of my being where I am known by God..." (3)

This is the essence of genuine self-intimacy, that I am able to live with myself as one who is known, accepted and loved by God. This awareness enables one to value one's self as precious and worthwhile.

It doesn't require great explanation to appreciate that our ability to know and value ourselves before God is what gives us the freedom to be intimate with another. The quality of my own self-intimacy will be reflected in the quality of my intimacy with others. This was most evident in Jesus' life and ministry.

But for us who struggle to value ourselves and know the truth of our being, we tend to relate less intimately and more in self-absorption. We tend to live in greater isolation than in self-giving, in deeper anxiety than in trust, more in fear than in freedom of spirit. Our struggle with intimacy may see us living more defensively and possessively and less in openness and generosity, in frustration and aggression rather than acceptance and respect and in greater insecurity than in confidence of being. The surest sign of our struggle with intimacy is when we live more in the dark and less in the light, when we live without a sense of reverence, without a sense of sacredness and mystery.

We know in our personal lives and in our own experience of ministry, the effects of our struggle to be more intimate. We hold back from others or we dominate them, we are on the defensive or we are threatened, we are critical and judgemental or we are non-communicative. However we express it, a lack of intimacy is perhaps one of the most undermining issues in our ministry today and indeed in our wider society.

a) The issue of abuse

In acknowledging my lack of authority on this subject I can only offer my sense that abuse, in any shape or form, whether it be sexual, physical, emotional or psychological, is somehow connected, and I suspect deeply connected with a lack of self-intimacy in the heart of the offender. If I do not respect my own being then how can I even begin to respect the being of another? We cannot give what we do not have nor what we have never known.

Without wanting to over simplify or treat in any superficial way the complexities of this matter of abuse, my intention in focusing on it here is to recognize that any matter that can devastate the heart and life of another person as deeply as this matter of abuse does, is a matter that cannot be overlooked or swept under the carpet. Abuse has happened and is happening in our Church. We cannot, as painful as it is, dismiss that fact nor can we ignore its impact upon our faith communities.

The impact of abuse upon some in our communities, is a growing sense of concern, mistrust, suspicion and caution. Things that we once took for granted in our relationships in ministry can no longer be assumed. People guard themselves and cover their tracks so that no misunderstandings will occur, no suspicion or accusations will be directed at them and no judgements will be made of them. This is leading to a lack of spontaneous warmth and genuine affection in some areas of ministry.

The problem will not go away by being over cautious or by guarding ourselves. Nor will we solve the matter by hard-headed denial, or cold-hearted legal battles. The problem is a problem of the heart. The hearts of the victims, the hearts of the offenders and the hearts of all of us who belong to this human Church are crying out for understanding, compassion and healing.

b) The issues of the law

But are the cries being heard or have we gone into our heads, wrenching ourselves further from our hearts? In many cases we do not admit our mistakes and own our failures. Instead we create further heartache for all involved through legal wrangling that may or may not bring about financial compensation and which, in the end, may or may not be fair and just.

Today people are suing and/or being sued excessively, not just for abuse but for almost everything! We have lost balance and perspective. There is no doubt that justice needs to be served and if the law enables that to happen, especially in the case of abuse, then well and good. But let us not deceive ourselves that the matters of the heart will be resolved in court rooms. Far from it. The law will not bring about the healing of the heart. In some cases it may be a good first step towards justice and healing, but often much more is needed.

Our Church is in desperate need of understanding on all sides, of compassion, healing and forgiveness. The wound has cut deeply and the judgements fall more harshly because today we are more informed, more is expected of us. Today, more than ever, we are being asked to validate the God we proclaim and today, people will not be satisfied with anything less from us.

The cries that surround the issue of abuse and other issues of injustice, are challenging us to a more genuine intimacy. This requires more serious personal formation for all involved in ministry, especially those in our leadership. The time is well overdue for us to put our energy and resources into forming ourselves and each other in the matters of the heart, in personal growth, in healing and reconciling, understanding and compassion, in restoring dignity and true justice.

It is time to recognise that the real problems facing our communities are heart problems, things that pertain to people's sense of worth and dignity, to their relationships and their sense of equality and justice. These things cannot be resolved in court rooms as effectively as they can be resolved in the painful struggle towards healing, reconciliation and forgiveness.

Our long overworked patriarchal and authoritarian approach has failed us terribly. In too many places this approach has invested all its energy into holding its structures together, even when they are obviously collapsing, rather than heeding the cries, healing the wounds, discerning the signs and finally, letting the structures fall graciously so that new and life-giving structures may emerge.

Surely it is time to embrace a new approach? It is Jesus' approach that needs to be embodied in our Church today.

With this as the backdrop of our concerns and issues in this area of ministry, let us move on to address the implications of Jesus' intimacy and affectivity in relation to our own ministry.

2. FOSTERING SELF-INTIMACY

If Jesus' warmth, affection and intimacy teach us anything, it is that we need to be in touch with ourselves and with our God in order to give the best of ourselves. The challenge here for us is to become more self-aware, more in touch with who we are and what we are on about, more at home with ourselves.

Because we are entrusted, in different ways, with people and their lives, we need to be women and men of integrity. This means we need to really know our vulnerability, our weakness and our strength. We need to keep forming ourselves in deeper self-awareness.

This may mean at times some good spiritual direction or counselling or contact with a good friend who can challenge us and help us own our truth. Just as Jesus developed nurturing relationships in the friendships of individuals such as Mary, Martha and Lazarus as well as with His disciples especially John, we too need to open ourselves to the loving friendship of others who will support us personally, and in turn, enrich our ministry.

The key to genuine self-intimacy is the personal realization that, as St. Augustine said, our hearts are restless until they come to rest in God. (4) The truly intimate heart is the one that rests in God and from that place of resting is free to relate authentically to others.

3. FOSTERING RIGHT RELATIONSHIPS

a) Intimacy, warmth and affection in our ministry

At a time when in some of our communities we most need to embrace each other, many are stepping back from each other and ministering from a distance. Given the above mentioned issues this is not surprising. Some people have become hesitant and inhibited in what were once spontaneous gestures of affection and warmth in ministry. The reluctancy to touch a child or a colleague, or the caution around being left alone with a student or parishioner has some of us distracted from the needs and concerns of those who come to us. While we do need to be sensible and in touch with what is happening we cannot hope to honour the God of Jesus by distancing ourselves or failing to promote loving relationships.

The right relationship in ministry is the one that is authentic and sincere, not going beyond one's own limits, not trying to express one's self as others do or as others would expect us to, but always relating out of one's own truth. Its expressions of warmth and affection are acceptable because they are genuine, they come from a heart that is in touch with itself and with the other. They are acceptable because they are respectful of the readiness, culture and personality of the individual. Not everyone for example, likes to be hugged or to hug others, because they are not openly affectionate by nature, or culturally it is not their way.

One's ability to accept such individual personalities and differences is in itself a warm and tender gesture. In such cases it is a matter of finding other ways to communicate warmth and affection. It is not always about physical touch. An expression of warmth and affection may be a smile or the tone of our voice. It may be in our body language or in our silence. It may be in a tender look or simply in our presence that we can communicate warmth and affection to another.

The challenge is to find the way that is right for each of us and for the other involved, recognizing that everyone is different. What is appropriate with one child or one particular parishioner may be completely inappropriate with others. The key here is to be present to our people so that we are in touch with them, as well as being present to ourselves and in touch with what is happening within us.

If we are serious about honouring the God of love whom we proclaim, then somehow, each in our own way, we need to embody the warmth and tenderness of God in the way we relate in our ministry and in our own personal lives.

b) Aware of the law

As much as we may think the lawsuit era is getting out of hand, the reality is that the law is on the alert and more and more people are aware of their rights. Even little children can quote the law to us. We need to be sensible in this area. If we are unsure of a situation then we might need to go slowly and gently, maintaining our professionalism while still being warm and personable.

We need to know what the risks are and do the best we can to stay quietly aware of the law without being overly cautious. We need to find the balance here or the legal mentality will cripple our hearts, forcing us to be functional task-oriented people and drain from within our ministry the warmth, affection and intimacy which Jesus proved to be so vital in establishing God's Kingdom.

c) More of God: less of us

When people came into the Presence of Jesus, they knew they were in God's Presence. Is that the case in our ministry? How do we keep God as the centre of our ministry? This is a tough one for many reasons.

A natural response when we are shown warmth and affection by another is to hold onto the one who cares for us so warmly.

We can become attached and caught up in the one who meets our need.

When our presence touches another we need to remember that we are on sacred ground and that while we may know what is in our hearts and where we are coming from we cannot presume the same awareness for the other. The risk here is that sometimes, especially in those who are particularly hungry for affection and nurturing, dependency, infatuation and hero-type idealized relationships develop. We become the centre attraction and somehow the deeper longing for God is misplaced as a dependency on us.

The indications of this can be subtle or very obvious. We need to read the signs as best we can. If we suspect that dependency is developing or projection is happening we need to speak the truth as lovingly and as respectfully as we can. This is so delicate because often people who are attached to us are not aware of their projections and may feel deeply rejected by us in our efforts to free up the relationship.

The sad reality is that sometimes we learn too late about how to read the signs and address such situations. We need to be able to own our part in such relationships, learn from our mistakes and from our errors of judgement. We need to be able to forgive ourselves and each other. The challenge is to keep learning from our failure and continue to read the signs. Experience teaches us the importance of staying in touch with ourselves, naming the issues involved and keeping them up front. It teaches us to speak the truth in love and to stay grounded in God.

We may also need to disengage from the relationship or change or redirect some aspect of it. Involving another colleague may be of help here so long as the attachment is not transferred onto the colleague. As painful as it is for all involved, at some point the truth needs to be spoken and the one who is dependent needs to be supported and challenged to face the real issues.

No doubt, by virtue of His impact upon people, Jesus would have had to deal with this problem of attachment and dependency. How did He deal with it? It seems He remained centred in God and focused on His mission of establishing God's Kingdom. The problem for us is that we lose focus and balance. We can easily be flattered by the impact we have on others, by the apparent effectiveness of our ministry and by the esteem others have of us. The focus becomes us and not the God who makes all things possible in us.

What is critical here is the ability to stay close to the centre of one's being, to keep our hearts focused on God and on what God calls us to. This will enable us to be responsibly aware of the power of our own presence and its impact upon others. The challenge for all of us in ministry is to give to others from the depths of the God within us. In this way we will be less the centre and God will be the whole.

4. CREATING THE RIGHT ATMOSPHERE

The warmth, affection and intimacy of Jesus' ministry challenges us to look seriously at the atmosphere in which we proclaim God. So often, especially with children, who learn by experience, we proclaim a God of love while we ourselves are so impersonal and insensitive to those who are present. We often contradict the tenderness and love of God by the cold and sometimes harsh manner in which we present that God to our people.

When we proclaim God in our liturgy or in our faith development our ability to sit with our people, to meet their eyes, to be warm and comfortable with them, especially in small informal groups, can do so much in honouring the God we proclaim.

The God who embraced children for example, is not appreciated by reading about that God from the Bible, so much as sitting with our children in a sacred space and telling them the Good News stories about that God and doing what Jesus would do were He there with those children; meeting their eyes, speaking to their hearts and embracing them.

If God is as Jesus proclaimed God to be, warm, tender, loving and intimate, then we need to examine the whole manner in which we present that God; the physical environment as well as our own spirit and energy. *This is not to suggest that God is limited by our environment or subject to our ability to be warm and affectionate.* It is suggesting however, that such factors can sensitize and influence significantly the receptivity of our people to the God we proclaim. We will discuss this in greater detail in our next chapter.

The point to be made from all this is that as Jesus enfleshed the God of love and healing, in the warmth, affection and intimacy of His Presence, we too are challenged to do the same by our presence to those with whom we minister.

We will take some time now to reflect on the issues raised here, within the context of our own local community.

PART THREE: RESPONDING TO THE IMPLICATIONS

Personal Synthesis:

1. What feelings do these reflections stir in you?

2. What issues and concerns do they raise for you?

3. What insights would you like to add to these reflections?

4. What does it mean to you to befriend yourself? What is it that you need to accept and nurture within your self? How does your struggle to be more genuinely self-intimate express itself in your life?

5. How comfortable are you in this area of affection and intimacy? What is your most natural way of expressing warmth and affection in your personal relationships and in your ministry?

6. What have you learnt about yourself in the struggles you have experienced in your relationships? What patterns can you identify? What insights can you see about how you relate? What healing and forgiveness do you need?

7. In what way do you struggle to keep God as the centre of your ministry? How can you address this?

Scripture Reflection:

Take some quiet time to ponder the following texts.

The Healing of the Deaf Man (Mk 7:31–37)

The Woman with the Haemorrhage (Lk 8:40–56)

The Rich Young Man (Mk 10:17–22)

• To which of these encounters do you most relate? What is it about that particular encounter that speaks to you?

• Have you known the touch of Jesus? When did your know this? How did you experience it?

Have you ever sensed yourself to be "seen" and discovered by Jesus? When did you feel this? How did you experience it?

Have you ever experienced Jesus looking steadily at you and simply loving you? When have you experienced this? How have you known it?

• How does your longing for the touch of Jesus express itself in your life? What would you want Jesus to do for you if you were able to meet Him as the people in these gospel encounters met Him? Imagine that now and savour it in your heart.

For Group Sharing:

• Allow the group time to connect and gather before you begin discussing these questions. It is important to be aware of people's energy and readiness for what is to follow. In light of this, it may be more appropriate to be selective with these questions or even to disregard them and find another way for your group to respond to the implications.

1. Each share in some way with the group something of your own personal synthesis of these reflections.

2. What questions, concerns and issues do these reflections raise for you as a ministry team within your community?

3. As a team, how hospitable and approachable do you feel you are to those who come to you? How warm is the atmosphere of your community?

4. How evident is the centrality of God in your ministry? What might be blocking the Presence of God in some areas of your ministry?

5. How does the atmosphere in which you proclaim God reflect and honour the nature of the God of Jesus? What more can

you do to nurture genuine warmth and intimacy in your min-istry, especially in your liturgy, faith education and outreach?

6. Given the relevancy and immediacy to your community of the issue of abuse within our Church, discern, if necessary, an appropriate way to enable you to address this within your team and, if necessary, with your community.

7. What matters of the heart do you need to address within your team and within your community? What can be done to acknowledge and address these matters in such a way that understanding, compassion, healing and forgiveness may be realized in the hearts of all concerned?

RITUAL AND PRAYER

• The following are suggestions that may assist you in bringing your sharing to prayer. They are only suggestions and should not be considered in any other way. It would be better to create your own prayer and ritual than to rely on something that comes from outside your sharing.

Suggestions:

1. Create a sacred space and atmosphere of quiet and stillness within the group. Soften lights if necessary and play some quiet background music. Give people time to focus. Light a candle and place the Word and or relevant symbols within the centre of the group. Try to integrate into the sacred space something that has come from your sharing. Ensure that people are able to see the sacred focus, that they are com-fortable and ready to enter into the prayerful spirit of this time.

2. Having identified the matters of the heart that are impacting upon you and your community, prepare a simple ritual of healing and anointing that could be integrated into this prayer

time. This ritual will be effective in as much as people are ready for it and open to it. Symbols and gestures such as incense, oil and laying on of hands may be an effective way to ritualize the healing and anointing.

3. The following scripture may be appropriate:
    Mk 1:40–45
    Lk 8:40–48
    Jn 15:9–17
    1 Phil 1:3–5; 7–11
    1 Th 3:12–13; 5:23

4. Some of the following songs may be helpful (please refer to page 191 for location of songs):
    Gather Us (ARH)
    Healing Is Your Touch (ARH)
    Let Your Heart Take Comfort (BUH)
    By Waiting And Calm (BUH)
    Touch My Life (GOL)
    God of Our Journey (GI)
    All Praise Glory and Honour (ARH)

5. At the conclusion of your prayer, share a meal or a drink or something that will enable people to celebrate and de-brief.

CHAPTER 4

IMAGINATION, CREATIVITY AND SACRAMENTALITY

PART ONE: SCRIPTURAL REFLECTION

From the depths of His being, Jesus knew the gestation of a dynamic and profound creativity. What was the nature of His creativity and what impact did it have upon His life and ministry?

We could spend an entire book on this alone, for there is such richness in Jesus' creativity and with it, many implications for us. This whole area of creativity and ministry by virtue of its experiential nature is better workshopped than written about, better experienced than talked about. However, we will do the best we can with the medium we have here.

To begin, let us qualify our meaning of creativity so that it is clear that in relation to Jesus and His creativity we are not talking about

His story-telling ability, but about a creativity that goes well beyond such skills.

Creativity is in some way a dawning, a discovery or a striking experience that is usually non-verbal and or metaphoric, imaginative, intuitive and aesthetic, plunging one's being into the vulnerable sphere of the spontaneous, symbolic, mysterious, mystical and sacred. (1)

Rollo May says it is the "process of bringing something new into being" (2). John Foley describes the artist who gives birth to this process as a "mothering womb" wherein the creative conception resides, taking form and shape, growing and eventually birthing outward to its realization. (3)

As a dawning discovery, creativity is born out of the interplay between imagination and intuition wherein imagination conceives a notion and engages intuition in the task of revealing the discovery. Imagination and intuition inform and empower each other in the birthing of creativity. (4)

This creative consciousness belongs to the right hemisphere of the brain. While the left hemisphere of the brain specialises in speech, logic, cognitive reasoning, analysis and categorisation, the right hemisphere specialises in the imaginative, intuitive, symbolic, affective and aesthetic dimensions of consciousness. (5)

When we look at how Jesus ministered and related we see that Jesus had a remarkable balance between the left and right hemispheres of the brain and in this sense integrated into His ministry a wholistic and balanced approach.

We have seen in His ability to teach great crowds, to challenge the Scribes and the Pharisees and to engage in lengthy discussions such as that with Nicodemus (Jn 3:1–21), that Jesus was adept in His skills of logic and reasoning. Now we want to consider His ability in the realm of the imaginative, intuitive and symbolic.

To say that Jesus was creative because He told stories is really to understate the depth of His creativity. While His story-telling is certainly creative and very gifted it is by no means the measure of His creativity. But let us reflect here on His gift as story teller, by way of a stepping-stone toward a deeper consideration of His creative spirit.

Jesus had a tremendous ability to take the ordinary every day things, activities and customs of the life of the people He encountered and turn them into sacramental symbols and images which spoke to them of God and the things of God.

A grain of seed becomes, through Jesus' imagination, a symbol of death and life and will never be just an ordinary seed to a Christian. Nor will the birds of the air and the flowers of the fields be to the believer just simply birds and flowers, but rather, a constant reminder of their worth and dignity in God's eyes. Why even the hair on our heads will never be just a strand of hair because Jesus used it to let us know the extent of God's awareness of us and the attentiveness of God's care for us (Mt 6:25–35).

Let us reflect on the many and varied realities of ordinary life that Jesus used to communicate the Word of God to the people of His time. As we read through this list, note what instantly comes to mind, without thought and reflection, just a spontaneous awareness.

Sheep and shepherd, a measure of yeast, the lost coin, a treasure in the field, a farmer, darnel, a fishing net, unforgiving debtor, vineyard labourers, fig trees, wedding feasts and banquets, bridesmaids and oil lanterns, mustard seeds, salt, lamps and wineskins, crafty stewards, prodigal sons and waiting fathers, travellers and brigands, unscrupulous judges and importunate widows.

My presumption is that as you read through this list, some of them no doubt more than others, spoke to you of the nature of God and the values of God's Kingdom. How can this be?

The creative genius of Jesus as a story-teller was His ability to take what was relatable to the ordinary life of the people and place it in a context that allowed it to be what it truly was, shepherd, new wineskin, darnel, treasure, whatever, and by virtue of the *dialogue* between the object or character's *relatability* and its *context*, transform it into something more than it was. In this sense the shepherd becomes the visual image of God's all-embracing love and mercy, treasure becomes the image of God's Kingdom, wineskins become the symbol of new vision and new structures, the darnel the symbol of sin and destruction.

The creative action on Jesus' part is first His own ability to see into the heart of the symbol and then to place it so aptly into the context of His teaching that the symbol becomes a manifestation and revelation of that which it is not, but truly is for those who have the eyes to see and the ears to hear.

And what are the eyes that can see and the ears that can hear the meanings implicit in Jesus' parables and stories. They are the eyes and ears of imagination and intuition.

At times Jesus would introduce a story or parable with "Listen! Imagine!" (Mk 4:3). Often He would conclude a story or parable with , "Listen, anyone who has ears." (Mt 13:9). Jesus taught about God by engaging the imagination and intuition of His listeners. But only those with the capacity to listen and really hear, the capacity to imagine and really see were able to appreciate Jesus' meanings. This may well be why Jesus was so reluctant to explain the parables and why the explanation of them is more probably the after-word of the gospel writers than of Jesus Himself (Mt 13:18–23).

Understanding Jesus' meaning requires not logic so much as imagination, not analysis so much as intuition and an appreciation of the symbolic. Perhaps this is why the hard headed Scribes and Pharisees couldn't appreciate Jesus' meaning and truth? For one who had the eyes to see could for example, look at a shepherd in search of its lost sheep and immediately recognize an image of the God of Jesus. But the one who cannot see looks at the same scene and sees a foolish shepherd wasting his time while the other ninety nine sheep wander off.

Jesus was able to transform these ordinary things and realities into sacramental symbols because Jesus could see into the heart of things. One of the qualities of intimacy discussed in chapter three was the capacity to uncover deeper meaning, to see the "more" that meets the eye. This ability is not just in relation to people, but indeed to all of life. Intimacy has a contemplative way of seeing the world, an intuitive wonder that can put us in touch with the inner nature of things. (6)

In this sense, Jesus was deeply intimate with His environment. He was finely attuned to life, able to pick up and connect readily to the inner meaning and deeper reality of His surroundings. His senses must have been sharp since He often used things of sight and sound to teach about God (Lk 12:54–56).

Jesus' ability to integrate these things of the senses so effectively into His teaching was one of His greatest gifts in His proclamation of God. He gave back to the people what He saw, heard, touched and felt of their lives, but in giving it back to them He had trans-formed it all, making of the simple and the ordinary, sacred symbols.

Jesus saw possibilities and new ways of approaching things. He had a healthy respect for the status quo and for tradition, yet He was quick to find another way. He shed new light on old laws, such as coming to terms with your neighbour before you get to court, or loving even one's enemy! With a fresh and uninhibited spirit He shifted and transformed old attitudes and mentalities and modelled a new way of seeing, of judging and of acting (Mt 5–7). The encounter with Zacchaeus is a fine example of this fresh approach by Jesus (Lk 19:1–10).

It was Jesus' ability to listen to and trust His intuitive spirit that enabled Him to be so creative in His ministry. He seemed able to get the measure of a person's heart very quickly and to know just how to respond to them (Jn 2:23–25). This is evident, for example, in the way Jesus responds to Pilate during His trial (Jn 18:28–40). Trusting one's instinct as deeply as Jesus did, is a risky business especially in regard to people and relationships. Jesus took some big risks in the way He dealt with certain people, especially the Scribes and Pharisees (Mt 23:1–36).

When our senses and instincts, our intuition and imagination are trusted and engaged often enough they become more finely tuned and more fully developed. If this happens faithfully then a person becomes an open vessel to inspiration and creativity. Such openness is a rich opportunity for grace to weave its way into our lives.

This is where we begin to appreciate something of the depth of Jesus' creativity. When we consider as we did in chapter three how Jesus healed people and brought about miracles in their lives, we notice in many cases how creative His action of healing was; how creatively inspired His miracles were.

When Jesus healed the blind man, for example, what possessed Him to take soil from the earth and mix it with His spittle into a paste and place it on the eyes of the blind man (Jn 9:6–7)? Was it an old wives tale of healing? Were there mysterious chemical reactions in the combination that brought about the healing? Or did Jesus do this by way of distracting from the sheer power of His touch, leading people to think that there was healing power in the action? And if there was healing power in the action then was it effused by Jesus somehow?

Even in the action of His transforming healing grace, which is in itself profoundly creative, Jesus exercises another level of creativity that makes it difficult to ascertain the difference between grace, creativity and miracles. Is there a difference?

We are not proposing here that Jesus worked miracles because He was creative. It is not a sense that Jesus' miracles came about through the power of His creativity. The suggestion here is that Jesus' creativity was so finely tuned to the inspiration of grace that in Jesus' embodiment of God's transforming power in the miracles He worked, Jesus engaged the whole of His creative being; intuition, imagination, intimacy, sensitivity, aesthetic and symbolic appreciation. In this sense Jesus' miracles are indeed a most creative act on the part of God.

If grace is the impacting of God's transforming spirit upon our human reality, and if that same grace inspires and empowers Jesus' creativity, which then becomes the means through which grace is embodied and expressed, then is it fair to conclude that Jesus' creativity was sacramental?

Jesus took ordinary bread into His hands in a way that bread had never been taken before. He blessed it and broke it as no other had blessed or broken bread and He gave it as His own life. Now that is creative!

We know that this is far more creative than the creativity that you and I would experience. In this Eucharistic action of Jesus we see that the depth of His creativity is nothing less than sacramental. Let us consider here this sacramental creativity of Jesus.

The whole setting and timing of the Eucharistic meal was, on the part of Jesus, sheer creative brilliance and magnificent sacramentality. How much of this was pre-planned by Him? The fact that He chose the place and made some preparations for this meal suggests that Jesus had a few things planned (Lk 22:7–13). How much had He planned? Did He know He was going to wash the feet of His disciples? Was this something that came to Jesus in the inspiration of the moment or did He deliberately choose to do this and for what reason?

In her dissertation on this powerful incident of the foot washing in John's gospel (Jn 13:2–15), Jill McCorquodale has proposed that Jesus' action of washing the feet of His disciples was a deliberate call to His followers to a new way of relating with Himself and each other. This new way was the way of mutuality, equality and deep communion; it was the way of friendship. This action made it clear that true discipleship and ministry were essentially about mutual love and friendship. (7)

Notice how Jesus teaches, not by word but by action. He gets down and He washes the dirty smelly feet of His friends. In doing so, He turned their culture upside down. Normally it was the task of the servant to wash the feet of guests, but here Jesus assumes the role of servant in such a dramatic way that the disciples are disturbed by it. Peter argues and resists. Jesus insists that they cannot be one unless Peter allows Jesus to do this. Jesus pleads with them "Do you understand what I have done?" Lord and God washing feet? Do *we* understand?

In washing their feet and in wiping them Jesus turns creative action into sacramentality; a sacred action and sign of God's trans- forming grace. In the creative conception and action of washing the feet of His disciples, so that they might know what ministry is truly about and go and do the same, Jesus sacramentalized mutual love and friendship. In this Jesus made the action the embodiment and experience of God's most reverent love and in so doing declared this to be the basis of all service and ministry.

Perhaps the washing of the feet needs to be our eighth sacrament? Perhaps it needs to be integrated more sacramentally by the creative action of *doing it* in our communities, especially in the formation and preparation of those involved in leadership and ministry?

Jesus' ability and effectiveness in integrating all the elements, the actions, the rituals, the symbols of this entire evening into the tra- ditional Passover meal reveals not only tremendous creativity but in that, a deep sense of intimacy.

Jesus, Luke tells us, was full of longing for this night (Lk 22:14–16). There were things, deep things that He wanted to say, things He wanted them to know and to understand? How much had He intuited about all that was to follow this meal? Did He know that this would be His last opportunity to speak His heart to them?

Jesus took one of the most revered celebrations and rituals of their religious tradition and turned it around so that the usual Passover symbols of salvation and God's blessing of mercy and love were not the focus in this Passover. Jesus, at some point had an extra-ordinary inspiration and revelation that His own life and blood would become for them the new covenant of love between God and God's people. The embodiment of that love would be bread and wine.

As Jesus took that bread and broke it and as He poured out that wine, He knew something that we will never understand; a self-giving and intimate surrender that is beyond our comprehension. He took the ordinary simple things of their lives, bread and wine and transformed them into His very life, given up, broken and poured out. Still the bread and wine remain what they appear to be, bread and wine, but to the believing heart they are sacrificial love and Presence.

So how did Jesus teach the disciples about the things that mattered so deeply to Him, the things that He so desperately wanted them to understand? There was an urgency in Him for them to grasp what His life and mission had really been about, so He washed feet and He broke bread. But did they understand? Would they be able to really go and do as He had done to them?

Jesus had to teach His followers in the best possible way, not just for their own understanding but for the life of the world. If they didn't understand then all that Jesus' had done might be wasted, come to nothing at all, die with Him. He was desperate for them to understand and do the same.

So He taught them sacramentally, in gesture, in action, in embodiment. He taught them creatively in intimate relationship. He taught them so that what He did and what they experienced with Him would be a *living memory* imprinted forever, not just on their minds and not just in their hearts, but lest they forget, experienced in their bodies!

Jesus taught and formed those disciples so well in the mutual love and friendship of genuine service and ministry that whenever they felt water on their feet, or saw and smelt the dirt of their feet, they might remember. In remembering they might experience again what they knew then and they might understand more deeply. In that understanding, they would go and do the same for each other.

Jesus' teaching and formation of those disciples was so effective that every time they took bread and wine in their hands they would remember that meal on that sacred night. In remembering, they would do what He had done. In doing what Jesus had done they would taste and know what they knew together there with Him; self-giving love and abiding Presence.

Because Jesus taught them so well, we are today, in our own way, able to understand what Jesus did and the meaning of His actions. The mark of our understanding will be, as it was for those first disciples, our ability to go and do the same.

In and through His creative sacramentality, Jesus honoured the creative tradition of Yahweh. In the biblical tradition of the Hebrew scriptures, which was immensely rich in story, imagery and symbol, Yahweh often spoke through the prophets in visions and dreams, and by inspirations that would come unexpectedly to them. (8)

Just as Jesus was inspired in His communication of God's Kingdom by what He saw and heard, so too the prophets who went before Him would see things in their ordinary circumstances that would inspire their proclamation of God. It might be the sight of an almond branch (Jr 1:11), or a visit to the potter's house (Jr 18:1–4), or noticing dry bones (Ez 37:1–14), or the experience of a gentle breeze (1K 19:9–14). The prophets before Jesus used many creative ways to convey their message. They used poems, love songs, parables, proverbs, satire, story and even mime.

The prophet Ezekiel's symbolic mime of the Exile, for example, was used by Yahweh to communicate to Yahweh's people, the nature of their desert wanderings in their exile (Ez 12:4–6). In another example, the prophet Nathan skilfully uses a story to call King David to accountability and repentance over his sins (2 Sam. 12:1–7).

Jesus not only honoured this rich creative scriptural tradition, He was the actual fulfilment of it. The Word was never more creatively expressed as it was in Jesus, for in Him the Word became flesh and dwelt among us (Jn 1:14). In Jesus the Word was, as the disciple John so beautifully expressed it, something that they saw and heard, something that they touched and felt. In Jesus the Word was living (1Jn 1:1).

God's purpose and intention in uttering the Word was perfectly fulfilled in Jesus. What was the purpose of God's Word? It was that it be flesh in our midst, living, dynamic Presence; that it penetrate our minds and our hearts, cutting more finely than a double-edged sword into the fibre of our being (Heb 4:12–13). The purpose of God's Word was that it seduce us, causing us to submit to it, accept it and do what it says (Jm 1:21–22). The purpose of the Word is, as Jesus Himself said, that it make its *home* within us (Jn 15:4).

Jesus fulfills every purpose and intent of God through His creative sacramental Presence, through His stories, images, symbols and, ultimately, by His death on the cross.

Let us move on to consider the implications of Jesus' creative ministry in the reality of our own ministry.

PART TWO: IMPLICATIONS

An appreciation of the nature and scope of Jesus' creativity and its integration into His ministry gives us a firm foundation upon which we can examine our own creativity and its place in our ministry. Again, this is more effectively addressed and appreciated in the experience of it rather than in writing about it.

1. APPRECIATING CREATIVITY IN OUR OWN LIVES

a) Creativity as a way of being

As we discussed earlier, the creativity we are concerned with here is not so much about talents and skills but about one's capacity to embrace their imagination, intuition and inner inspiration.

Particular gifts and talents in the Arts and other creative expression are a blessing and may well be a bonus, but they are not the kind of creativity we are primarily concerned with here. Individuals may be brilliant in their skills and technique but may lack the creative heart that is so critical to ministry.

Our most valuable creativity is not invested in talent and skills but in an attitude of heart, in a way of being, in a stance before life. If we believe that we are made in the image and likeness of our God, then we need to accept that we are creative in being. To deny our creativity is to deny the truth of our being in God.

The reality is, that for many of us, we have not nurtured or developed our creativity, we have relied too heavily on our heads and have failed to attend to our hearts. Where once the creative language was our most natural language, the older we become it seems to become more a foreign language for us, a language that we are not only unfamiliar with but uncomfortable with.

The personal challenge for all of us in our own lives and in our ministry, is to reclaim what we have lost and nurture what we have neglected within our creative spirit. It is about recognizing that we have more than a head and mind with which to reason and know reality. We have a heart and a body that together can know infinitely more of what really matters in life than our minds could comprehend.

Reclaiming our natural creative language is about having ears that really hear and eyes that really see, developing a sensitivity to the things that surround us and the movement within us. It is about listening, imagining, seeing, believing, daring and risking. This is the real stuff of our creativity.

b) Self-intimacy and creativity

To the extent that we are able to live with ourselves, to be at home with who we are, to accept and trust our inner movement, in particular, our intuition and imagination, to that extent will we be able to honour our creativity.

Jesus' life and ministry validate the truth of this. He was an open vessel through which His creativity flowed so abundantly and with such richness. He was able to trust His inner movement. He could see into the depth of things and trust what He saw and knew. His highly developed intuition empowered Him to find another way, to see new possiblities and to take risks.

This is the challenge for us. It all hinges on our ability to be self-intimate. Our problem is we battle with ourselves rather than accept who we are. We barely listen to, let alone trust, our imagination and intuition. We feel safer and more in control in our heads, less likely to take any risks that could fail in some way, or expose us in any way! This is particularly evident when it comes to any physical expression of our creativity.

For many of us our greatest struggle around creativity is our fear of our bodies. We are generally not at home with our bodies and live most of our lives rejecting and resisting them in their needs, desires and potential. We do not dare to use our bodies in creative process for fear that we might be seen. We feel the butterfly flutter grow into a huge tight knot in our centre as we get up to say or do something, hoping that no-one, especially our peers and colleagues, will notice us.

All of this is, I believe, symptomatic of our struggle with intimacy. We dread any form of disclosure and by virtue of its nature, creativity is dependent in one way or another on disclosure, whether it be a word, a thought, an idea, a possibility, a gesture, a sound, a movement.

Whatever the creative movement, we fear that in giving expression to it, it may be rejected and we might feel foolish. This fear of rejection is so painful because what we have disclosed and shared comes not from a book or a resource outside us, but it comes from somewhere deep within us. The creative rejection is so painful because we experience it as a rejection or failure of *who we are*. This is, I sense, one of the main reasons why adults, particularly, can be so threatened by creative language and process.

Deep sensitivity and respect are required here. Creative process that by-passes people's readiness and creates stress and anxiety, embarrassment and undue pressure is not genuine creativity. It is an atmosphere and spirit of respect and reverence, affirmation and support that will promote freedom in our creative expression. If the creative expression is to be sacramental, life-giving and enriching, then anything less than this spirit of reverence will block the flow of grace.

A sure way to ease the threat and fear that we can experience around creativity and come to a liberating freedom in it, is to embrace ourselves in self-accepting love. This will not happen because we tell ourselves or someone else tells us to do so. This is not a matter of instructing but of *living in relationship*, at times painfully so, with others and with our own inner being where God is mysteriously present.

We may need to appreciate at some stage, that the struggle for self-acceptance is not exclusively an emotional or psychological concern but ultimately it is a concern of faith. Do we know and do we believe in who we are before God? As simplistic as this may sound, the essence of it is that God is the one who knows me in all my brokenness and beauty. In God I may find the truest and surest relationship in which to discover my own beauty and creativity. This may enable me, perhaps simply in the comfort it gives me, to befriend myself a little more, and this will in turn, enable me to be more open to developing life-giving relationships with others.

Ultimately it is love that nourishes our creativity, because in love there is the real stuff of life. It is not just the joy and wellbeing in love that feeds and frees our creativity, it is also the pain, the heartache and the suffering that can, strangely enough, enrich it.

Suffering leads us down the dark passages of life. In the depths of the broken spirit creative inspirations can germinate, having been fuelled by our desolation and by the failure of our head and logic to deal with the reality or to find a solution.

Suffering forces us, if we are to survive, to dig deep, to discover new and deeper places in our hearts from which creative energy springs forth, just as the seed buried in the earth brings forth new life from its death. Here our imagination and intuition can lead us out from the depths of despair giving us the notion of a way through the darkness. In this way creativity becomes liberation, pointing us to the vision of the new dawn yet again.

2. THE ROLE OF CREATIVITY IN MINISTRY

a) Creativity and the experience of God

We have already discussed the centrality of the experience of God as personal, intimate Presence in spirituality and religious experience. We have proposed that it is the experience of God as relatable Presence that gives meaning and vitality to our theology, catechesis, ritual and liturgy. What contribution, if any, does the creative process make in providing opportunity for our people to experience God in their lives?

There is nothing rational or logic, by virtue of God's nature, about the experience of the mystery of God. The language with which we express and communicate our sense of God is not the language of analysis or reason. So much of what we know and do and say in relationship to God is beyond words and makes little if any "head sense".

The language that best honours the nature and experience of God is the language of symbol, image, imagination and intuition. (9) God's communication is, as we have seen in Jesus and in the prophets before Him, expressed through the imagination. Grace actually impacts upon our reality in symbolic and aesthetic language. Andrew Greeley clarifies this for us,

The experience of grace is an impact on the senses and then is filtered through the imagination where it has an enormous and sometimes overwhelming effect. Even long after the experience is over the residue remains in the imagination, capable of recollection and of exciting once again resonances of the experience. (10)

Creative language is the most natural language for the soul because it understands and resonates with the nuances of mystery and Presence. It verbalises, expresses and articulates through images, symbol, movement, colour, shape and sound the movement and Presence of God in our lives. John Westerhoff believes that,

...religion belongs to the sphere of the unsayable, the absurd, the world of nonsense, which if it is to be put into words at all we must use metaphorical images, symbolic words and poetry. Religion is better sung than recited, better danced than believed, better painted than talked about. (11)

The soul is vulnerable to the imaginative, intuitive, metaphoric and aesthetic language, for this language penetrates, stirs and nourishes the soul by what the soul sees, hears, touches, feels, witnesses, experiences in the communication of this creative language.

As we saw in Jesus' ministry, when creative language is well used it can be sacramental, transcending what is human and opening up to the divine. In this sense creative language is like the burning bush at Moses' feet. It helps us know that we are on holy ground, that the sacred is in our midst (Ex 3:1–6). It provides us with the means to communicate with and respond to God, to honour and reverence the Sacred One present in our midst.

The experiential things that we see and hear, touch and feel, in image and symbol, have the potential, as did Jesus' action of washing feet and breaking bread, of teaching us in a most impressionable manner of the things of God. These are the things that become written on our hearts, residing within us as living transforming memory.

b) Integrating creative language in our ministry

Had Moses become fixated on the burning bush he may never have experienced his God. The bush itself was not God but the vehicle and means through which God communicated. In this same sense the creative act itself is not an end in itself, but in this context of the experience of God, it is the means to the end.

Once the creative gesture becomes fixated as an end in itself, existing for the affective stimulation it provides, then that is precisely all that it will be, an affective stimulant. It is on this basis that many argue against the use of the arts in spirituality, especially in liturgy and prayer, claiming that they do nothing more than distract from the real centre, and at worst, desecrate what is sacred.

There is no doubt that in some situations that is the case. Anything that is poorly presented or improperly applied can be detrimental to our worship and prayer. When it comes to something as sacred as our liturgy and the proclamation of God's Word, only the very best efforts we make are worthy. By "best effort" we are not meaning perfection of performance but sincere, heartfelt embodiment. This will be discussed further in our last section.

The greater obstacle to an effective integration of the creative in our ministry, is the rationalistic mind-set that too easily dismisses the value and worth of the imaginative and aesthetic in religious experience. Amos Wilder has a direct and challenging message to that mind-set. He insists that imagination has to,

...defend itself on the one hand against a pragmatic no-nonsense type of mentality, representing a kind of devastated area in a culture whose aesthetic and spiritual antennae have been blighted. In this camp are also rationalists and religious dogmatists for both of whom experience lacks its deep creative registers...On this front any plea for religious imagination opens the critic to the charge of mere aestheticism. His concern appears to be fanciful or frivolous. But the charge of aestheticism is all too often a defensive ploy to protect some conventional security or lifestyle. (12)

This is where the creative question becomes an issue of contention and frustration, and in some communities of division and anger. This is in itself a contradiction of the very nature of creativity. What is required here is a change of heart and a shift of attitude. Somehow all perspectives need to be appreciated and respected. There needs to be a sincere effort to address and resolve the tensions before there can be any real creative expression in our worship and prayer.

Wilder goes on to echo what Rahner has previously stated, that religious experience, and in particular liturgical experience, by virtue of its symbolic nature, loses its vitality, becomes conceptual, theoretical and deadened when it relies on heady theologizing and verbal discourse. God is not a matter for the head but an experience of the soul, not a theory to be taught but *Presence to be experienced.*

...Imagination is a necessary component of all profound knowing and celebration, all remembering, realising and anticipating; all faith, hope and love. When imagination fails doctrines become ossified, witness and proclamation wooded, doxologies and litanies empty, consolations hollow, and ethics legalistic. (13)

God will not be honoured by rituals and worship that separate the head from the heart or worse still, alienate the heart. Neither will God be honoured in an over indulgence of the symbolic and imaginative. The most worthy way to honour God in our liturgy and worship is by holding all in balance, recognizing the true value of moderation and simplicity. In the end we need to remember, as William Johnston reminds us that,

God is unlike anything we know. We must keep in mind that the ideas we have of God are totally inadequate to contain God (14)

A balanced integrated approach to creativity may allow us the opportunity not to contain God, but to ponder and wonder, question and search out the mystery of God in our lives. At best it may provide us with a language with which to celebrate and reverence our God, a language with which to respond to God in our lives.

The creative operation of God does not simply mould us like soft clay. It is a fire that animates all it touches, a spirit that gives life. So it is in living that we give ourselves to that creative action, imitate it, and identify with it. (15) We become co-creators, more than just the created.

c) *Creative language and the Word of God*

Can we assume, given the nature and purpose of God's Word, as mentioned in an earlier section, that the Word is relevant and meaningful in the lives of our people, whether they be children, youth or adults? Can we assume that the Word is in fact fulfilling its purpose in their lives? Is the Word penetrating their hearts and minds, challenging and calling forth new life, seducing their false reality, causing them to submit, to change and to do what the Word says? Is the Word making its home in the lives of our people? Is it making its home in our own lives?

The truth is we can assume nothing when it comes to the Word in the life of another. But generally speaking, it is more likely that to varying degrees for many of our people, as indeed for some of us, the Word of God is experienced as being distant from and irrelevant to our lives. For some, much of the Word is too familiar and its impact is not realized. For others it is unfamiliar and its meaning and richness eludes them.

Jesus came to make the Word flesh in our midst. But do we see the Word, do we really hear it , do we touch it and feel it in the circumstances of our lives? That we proclaim the Word from our lecterns or read from our bibles and pronounce it as "The Word of God", does not make it the living Word in the daily circumstances of our people's lives.

In our tradition, Mark Coleridge says the Word "stands at the heart of the divine communication" (16). Is it central to our lives? How can we provide opportunities for our people that enable the Word to fulfil its purpose in their lives?

A deeper appreciation of the inherent creative nature of the Word may assist us in our proclamation of the Word. Bausch maintains that,

The scripture, dealing as it insists with God and mystery, must take the form of story, with story's natural expressions of epic, legend, poetry, myth, metaphor and all other ways that it intends to supply, not information, but meaning, inspiration and commitment. (17)

Scripture is a creative feast, using imaginative, symbolic and dramatic language and needs to be proclaimed in a manner befitting its nature.

Proclaiming the Word creatively is not just about applying mime or dance, symbol or dramatic presentation, although when this is well done it can be a powerful proclamation of the Word. However, this is only half the process. We need to do what Jesus did, embody the Word by connecting with our people and breaking the Word open with them, in response to and in relationship with their lives and their story. In this way the Word is in dialogue with their reality, just as it was for those who sat in the crowds and hung on every word Jesus proclaimed, because it was *their* story of life and somehow Jesus knew it and was part of it.

This means for us a deeper awareness of our people. It means sometimes sitting with them and dialoguing with them around their stories and God's story, providing them with perhaps nothing more than the time and space and maybe a good measure of silence, wherein God can do what only God can do, speak to their hearts.

Breaking open the Word is about coming into the heart of the Word to find that its meaning is our life. Breaking open the Word is about enabling our people to ask questions of the Word, to ponder it, grapple with it and explore its images and symbols. It is about discovering what the Word reveals about the person of Jesus. Engaging the imagination and intuition of our people, may assist them, in allowing the Word to reveal its meaning and richness to them, allowing it to make its home within them.

Benedictine women and men throughout the world have a rich appreciation of what it means to ponder the Word. In the Benedictine tradition of spirituality, it is called Lectio Divina, a gentle, pondering, mulling over and inner listening to the Word. It is not an exegesis of the Word, nor is it approached as an exercise of one's intellect. Pondering the Word is about listening to the Word and attending to it with the ear of one's heart.(18) This is the listening that allows one's soul to be receptive to the nuance of the Word.

Our role here in providing opportunity for such pondering, is that of enablers, facilitators, even mid-wives in the sense that we provide the atmosphere and the supportive process for our people to experience the birthing of God's Word in their lives, through the struggle, pain, joy, even bliss of it all, engaging the whole of their being.

This requires much more of us than does our usual pattern of teaching the Word. We cannot, for example, expect that because we tell our people the Word is life, and meaningful and relevant, that they will experience it to be that because of our authority or scholarship. We cannot make meaning relevant to anyone in that sense. Meanings become relevant when they are validated by experience, as we have seen in Jesus' ministry.

Being facilitators and enablers of the Word by providing opportunity and processes for our people to experience the meaning of the Word is far more demanding of us personally. It means we cannot just hand out notes to our adults or photocopy pictures of Jesus for our children to colour in and expect that the Word will be relevant to them. We need to engage the whole of their senses so that the Word is seen, is really heard, is touched, is felt, is experienced by them.

This means for us that, above all, we need to have grappled with the Word. We need to have questioned it and pondered it so that we are at home with the Word and the Word is at home in us. This simply means that we have a sense of comfort, wellbeing and authenticity in the Word that we proclaim.

In ways that are authentic for each of us, we need to reclaim the rich creative biblical tradition of Yahweh and of Jesus, in the way we proclaim and break open the Word of God. We need to develop, explore and engage our creative language of imagination, intuition, symbol and image in ways that will provide opportunity for the Word to fulfil its purpose in our lives and in the lives of those to whom we minister.

In the prophet Isaiah, Yahweh makes it clear that the Word will not return to God without fulfilling God's purpose; that is without it watering the desert of our human lives and sensibilities, without yielding and giving growth to the seeds of new meaning, new possibilities, new hope and new life in our hearts. The Word will not fail to honour in some way God's purpose in our lives (Is 55:10–11).

d) Practical issues involved in integrating creative language in ministry

If we are going to be effective in our integration of creative language in our ministry we may need to develop a certain kind of sensitivity and intuition that enables us to discern what is appropriate and what is not and how best to carry out the process or experience.

This special kind of sensitivity and intuition is often the vital link which can make or break an experience. In something as sacred as our liturgy, every possible support needs to be given to ensure that what we are doing and involved in honours and enhances our ritual and sacramentality and in no way deters from it.

Here are a few hints or suggestions that have come out of years of trying to honour this creative way of ministry. You will have your own experience to add to this and that is the experience that is critical here.

Knowing our people and their readiness is perhaps the most critical issue here. To push and challenge our people beyond their creative threshold, especially in a liturgical setting, is an abuse of both the creative act and of our people's trust. But inviting and leading them through rituals and process that accept their readiness, can bring about genuine participation and response. This may mean taking very small steady and sure steps in integrating a more creative approach to our ministry. If the relationship is right, genuine and mutual, creativity flourishes! We can call forth so much from our people if we have good relationships with them.

Attending to the finer details of timing, placement, preparation, presentation, atmosphere and setting can contribute to the overall effectiveness of our creative gesture. Anything that is too much or too little, too fast or too slow, too loud or too soft, too strong or too weak can take from the effectiveness of what we do. Balance and simplicity are the key here.

Recognizing the difference between performance and embodiment is so important in integrating the Arts in our ministry, and in particular in our liturgy. Performance may be technically brilliant but leaves our hearts cold. What is the difference? It is not the technical and professional capacity of the artist that is the problem so much as where it is coming from within the artist. It is what directs, inspires and motivates a presentation that will determine its impact upon us.

Having a feel for the sacred is what makes the difference; that is, a sense of presence, of reverence and openness to the inspiration and movement of God's grace at work in us. We know there is a difference between performance for its own sake and performance which embodies the sacred, simply because we *feel* the difference.

In using symbols and rituals we need to be aware of what Jesus knew so well, that their effectiveness is in their relatedness to people's lives. We have so many rich symbols in our tradition, too many of which have been long forgotten. In integrating them in our ministry we may need to highlight them in a way that enables their true symbolism to speak to us. It may mean reflecting on them in some way, breaking them open, and exploring their meanings with our people before we use them sacramentally.

We may need to remember that if a symbol is a true symbol it will mean different things to different people. There are no right or wrong appreciations of symbols. But symbols that are too literal or over explained will limit the breadth and the depth of their creative and sacramental capacity.

Finally, in integrating creative language in our ministry we need to acknowledge that people have preferred ways of knowing and doing, of communicating and expressing, of celebrating and praying. Not everyone, as we have mentioned earlier, is at home with or even interested in creative expression.

It is important that our creative language integrate, as much as possible, the different ways of communicating; that is verbal, audible, visual and physical. Essentially this is concerned with finding a balance between our heads and our hearts so that neither is dominated or neglected but in mutual dialogue with each other. This is, in itself, a real art and a most powerful creative language.

Let us consider what all this means within our local community.

PART THREE: RESPONDING TO THE IMPLICATIONS

Personal Synthesis:

1. What feelings do these reflections stir in you?

2. What issues and concerns do they raise for you?

3. What insights would you like to add to these reflections?

4. How comfortable are you with your own creativity? Where and how does it express itself in your life? How can you nurture and develop your creativity?

5. What do you fear or resist around your creativity, in your own personal life and in your ministry?

6. How at "home" are you with the Word of God? When has the Word been made flesh in your life? What enabled this to happen for you?

Scripture reflection:

Take some quiet time to ponder the following text.

The Washing of the Feet (Jn 13: 2-15).

• Imagine yourself as one whose feet is washed by Jesus. Visualize the details of this: the water..., the touch..., the feeling..., the whole sense of it.

• What would you find challenging about having your feet washed by Jesus? What would such an experience mean for you? What would you learn about yourself? What would you learn about Jesus and your relationship with Him?

• What does Jesus' directive to go and do the same challenge you to do?

Group Sharing:

• Allow the group time to connect and gather before you begin discussing these questions. It is important to be aware of people's energy and readiness for what is to follow. In light of this, it may be more appropriate to be selective with these questions or even to disregard them and find another way for your group to respond to the implications.

1.   Each share in some way with the group something of your own personal synthesis of these reflections.

2.   What questions, concerns and issues do these reflections raise for you as a ministry team within your community?

3.   How does Jesus' creativity challenge you as the ministry team within your community? What can you learn from it?

4.   How does your community express its creativity? Who are your artists and your creative initiators and enablers? Are their gifts being integrated into the life of your community? In what way?

5.   What are some of the difficulties and tensions for you and your community around this issue of creativity? What can be done to address these difficulties and tensions?

6.   When have you experienced the sacramentality of creativity in your community? What enabled this experience to be sacred?

7.   How can you, as a ministry team, be more aware of the value of creative language and its contribution to the life of your community?

8.   How relevant do you believe the Word of God is to the people in your community? Can you identify, in a general way, those who may struggle with the Word of God? What is one initiative you could implement that would enable your community to experience the Word as a truly living Word?

RITUAL AND PRAYER

• The following are suggestions that may assist you in bringing your sharing to prayer. They are only suggestions and should not be considered in any other way. It would be better to create your own prayer and ritual than to rely on something that comes from outside your sharing.

Suggestions:

1. Create a sacred space and atmosphere of quiet and stillness within the group. Soften lights if necessary and play some quiet background music. Give people time to focus. Light a candle and place the Word and or relevant symbols within the centre of the group. Try to integrate into the sacred space something that has come from your sharing. Ensure that people are able to see the sacred focus, that they are comfortable and ready to enter into the prayerful spirit of this time.

2. Consider integrating into your prayer a ritual for washing the feet of your team members. This needs to be well prepared. People will need to be consulted and some will need to be reassured. The readiness of each person will need to be respected.

There may be other ways of achieving a similar end if the group are not ready to wash one another's feet. Washing one another's hands, for example, may be a less threatening experience for the group. Preparation of the setting, the atmosphere and all details of the ritual are critical to the sacredness of this ritual. It is better not to attempt this unless it is well planned.

3. The following scripture may be appropriate:
   Jn 13:2–15
   Jn 14:23–24
   Is 55:10–11
   Jm 1:21–25

4. Some of the following songs may be helpful (please refer to page 191 for location of songs):
    Gather Us O God (ARH)
    Speak Lord (ARH)
    Do You Understand (GOL)
    In Memory of You (ARH)
    To Whom Shall We Go (BUH)
    To the Glory of God (BUH)

5. At the conclusion of your prayer, share a meal or a drink, or something that will enable people to celebrate and/or de-brief.

CHAPTER 5

TIME ALONE, TIME WITH— TRANSFIGURATION

PART ONE: SCRIPTURAL REFLECTION

When one is so deeply engaged with the issues of life, as Jesus was in His own personal life and in His ministry, it is not in any way surprising to find frequent reference in the gospels to the time Jesus spent alone.

In the midst of His daily reality, often preceding or immediately following His experience with crowds of people, or encounters wherein miracles have occurred, Jesus would take Himself away to a quiet place where He could be alone.

In this chapter we want to take some quiet time ourselves to ponder what Jesus would have done in those times alone. What thoughts and feelings might have occupied His mind and heart?

What questions and concerns would He have grappled with? What soul searching would He have shared with His God? What would Jesus have experienced in His times of prayer?

In one sense these questions are ridiculous. Given that the nature of prayer is so personal, how could we dare to imagine anything of what Jesus' experience was like. It is hard enough for us to articulate our own experience of prayer, let alone attempt to know someone else's experience, and even more so, Jesus' experience! The most we can do is ponder, imagine, question and use the gospels as a guide for our wonderings.

It appears from the synoptic gospels that at some point soon after Jesus' baptism by John, Jesus withdraws to the wilderness (Mt 4:1–11). I sense that in some way the timing of this is most significant. The baptismal experience of Jesus must have been a powerful experience for Him.

All three accounts have recorded some form of mystical encounter between Jesus and the Spirit of God (Mt 3:16–17). How this actually was experienced by Jesus and perceived by others is a mystery. What is important, however, is that somehow Jesus knew in this baptismal experience that He was the Beloved and blessed of God. What did this mean to Jesus?

In Matthew's account of this experience, which appears to be the main reference for Mark and subsequently Luke's account, the word "servant" is replaced by "Son". The gospels, while declaring in this experience that Jesus was the anointed servant foretold by Isaiah, actually go further and declare Jesus to be "Son of God". (1)

What was Jesus' understanding of this baptismal experience? Is it in response to this experience that Jesus takes Himself out into the wilderness, perhaps to do some serious soul searching; perhaps to come to terms with His own identity in relationship to God? If He were "Son" then what did that mean for Him? What did it mean for

Him in relation to His mission and His understanding of His mission?

Whatever Jesus' intention was in going to the wilderness He certainly appears to have struggled and grappled with Himself. And what was the focus of His struggle? It appears to have been a fierce tussle between God's way and our human way of power, pride and self-importance; all the destructive and evil misconceptions we are tempted to believe about ourselves.

Surely Jesus, having experienced Himself to be the Beloved and blessed of God had to deal with these ego-centred temptations in a radical way. And isn't that exactly what wilderness is about; a desolate struggle within one's own being and the eventual survival and realization of what is most authentically of God in us?

It would seem that before Jesus dared to begin His ministry He chose to search out His soul in the wilderness experience. This was not to be a once-and-for-all experience, as we have already discussed. This soul searching and struggle to choose God's way was a temptation that remained with Jesus throughout His life.

The many occasions when Jesus slipped away long before dawn (Mk 1:35–36) could well have been times of more wilderness-type experiences for Him. They may have been times when, given the impact of His ministry, the crowds, the miracles, the talk about Him, Jesus needed to search His heart and soul before God to understand and hold onto the truth of His being and the purpose of His mission.

It was, according to the gospels, difficult for Jesus to get away from the crowds to be alone. Even when He had set out to do so, people would seek Him out, including His disciples, sometimes reprimanding Him because they had been looking for Him and could not find Him (Mk 1:36–37). How did Jesus feel when He was interrupted in those times when, being so desperate to be alone, He would rise very early before dawn or even spend the entire evening in prayer (Lk 6:12)?

Sometimes, having been discovered by His disciples, Jesus would set about teaching and forming them, surely out of the insights from His own prayer and from the nourishment He received in His time alone with God (Mk 4:10–11). Sometimes Jesus insisted that they all get away together where they could be alone, to rest and simply be, to think and reflect, to pray (Mk 6:31–33).

Perhaps it was in those times that questions would be asked, sometimes by the disciples and sometimes by Jesus. "Who do people say I am?" Why did Jesus ask this question? Was He curious about what people were saying about Him? Was it a genuine heartfelt, soul searching question for Jesus? Did Jesus need feed-back about how people were perceiving Him?

And why is it important that He hear from His friends what they think? "You", He says to them, "Who do you say I am?" Was it to test their faith? Or was this very direct question to His disciples who had become His friends, a time of mutual sharing and mutual searching? Was Peter's answer the articulation and declaration of faith that they each knew in their hearts but could not find words to express? Was this intimate faith sharing as much for Jesus as it was for the disciples (Lk 9:18–21)?

Many questions would have stirred in Jesus' heart in those times alone and with His disciples. "Do you understand," He would often ask His disciples, "what I have done?" And how did He feel when they didn't understand His meaning and His purpose (Mk 4:13)? And when they showed signs of comprehending, of under-standing, how did His spirit feel then (Mt. 13:16–17)?

Sometimes on their journey Jesus would let the disciples go ahead, planning to meet them elsewhere so that He could take sometime alone in prayer, often in the hills (Mt 14:22–23). And once alone what would Jesus do? There under the stars what questions did He ask of His God? Did He reflect back over the events of the day with God? Did He ever feel overwhelmed and in awe of what He had experienced in the crowds, with the people; what He had seen, heard, felt and even what He had done?

Did He wonder for example about the crippled woman and the hypocrisy of the synagogue official? And how about the little children, and what about the feeding of the five thousand, and then the woman who washed His feet with her tears? And what about the disciples arguing over which of them was the greatest, and John the Baptist being beheaded, and Lazarus' death and rising, and the disciples still not understanding? And how about the Pharisees harassing the man born blind and what about Mary anointing his feet?

Did Jesus turn to His God to fix His problems and resolve His concerns or did He turn to God out of sheer longing to be with the One who called Him Beloved? Did Jesus go to God simply as He was, at times exhausted, overwhelmed, silenced, in awe, full of gratitude? Did He go to His God sometimes frustrated, angry, fearful, confused and in need of direction? Did He go at times to His God full of longing, desire, restlessness, emptiness?

Was Jesus' heart heavy and aching at times? Were His thoughts distracted and disturbing at times? Did Jesus struggle with what we struggle with in prayer when we come to our God? Did Jesus feel alone at times and without the comfort of His God?

If Jesus took to heart what He was experiencing in His ministry then He surely would have taken it to God. Not in the sense that God was somehow separate from His daily reality, but in the sense of having time for inner deep listening, time for focusing one's life and its events and circumstances plainly before God, for discernment and guidance.

When Jesus saw the crowds coming to Him like sheep without a shepherd what would He have shared with God about that

(Mt 9:35–37)? And when He wept over Jerusalem and feared for its future what would He have prayed about in that (Lk 19:41–44)? When He healed the Gerasene demoniac and all those pigs stampeded down the cliff face, what did Jesus share about that with God (Mk 5:1–20)? And what about when His disciples were sending the children away and He chose to let them stay with Him and spend time with them? Did He delight in that with God (Lk 18:15–17)?

And when Jesus' disciples returned from their first mission and went off with Him so that they could share their experiences and tell their stories, how did He feel and what did He say to God about all that (Lk 9:10–11)? And when He lost His temper in the temple, when His rage at the corruption of the Pharisees and Scribes became too much for Him, how did He reflect on that in His prayer (Jn 2:13–17)?

Did Jesus get angry with God as we do? Did He blame God as we do? Did He delight and rejoice with God about certain things that were happening? Did He tell God what should have happened and what needs to happen? Did He sit in the dark in long silences trying to come to terms with the things He experienced? Did He know the deep stillness of intimate Presence with His God? Did Jesus ever wonder what was happening to Him and in Him in relation to God and His ministry?

If the Agony in the Garden was in any way typical of how Jesus prayed then we can assume that His prayer was very real, for what we sense in this agonizing experience of Jesus is nothing less than raw human struggle (Lk 22:39–46). The fear is not hidden, the anguish is not disguised. Here is a man groping to avoid the darkness that engulfed Him. Jesus is gripped by an urge to run from the pain, to say no to what God is allowing to happen to Him. His cry is a desperate cry and His pleading with God that the darkness would pass Him by is heartfelt.

But surrender comes. The wrestling is all done. Jesus at some point in this agony lets go. We sense a resolution in Him to embrace whatever is before Him.

The movement in this prayer of Jesus from fear and resistance to acceptance and surrender is not, I would imagine, a movement that is unfamiliar to Jesus. My sense is it is the pattern of a heart that many times has struggled and pained to give over fully to God and God's way.

This is not the kind of surrender one chooses so much as allows. The surrender that Jesus knew is the surrender that *happens* in one's soul when love breaks through fear and all resistance dissolves. It is the surrender that *happens* at that moment when the God of love overwhelms fear and resistance with Presence that simply can no longer be resisted. Here surrender is not about will but about love, consummate love.

Perhaps the more one experiences this surrender the more vulnerable one becomes to it. If one's soul is familiar with this vulnerability then the more readily Love will find its mark and have its way. The more Love finds its way in our souls the more it will overcome all that frustrates its desire, until the surrender is so complete it submits even to death!

And so it does. The movement is there again in Jesus, on the cross, where the pain and despair of abandonment give over to complete and utter surrender, "Into your hands I commend my spirit" (Lk 23:46).

Jesus would not have been predisposed or susceptible to the complete surrender of the cross unless His whole life had been familiar with this pattern and movement of surrender. His experience of transfiguration may well have been a most critical moment in this pattern in relationship with His God.

We will never know clearly what happened in Jesus in this transfiguration experience. In ways that are beyond our comprehension, Jesus must have been so totally present to the God who claimed Him, yet again, as Beloved, that somehow beyond words, somehow in endless space, in timeless moment, Jesus was immersed in His God so deeply that His very appearance was transfigured.

What did this experience do to Jesus? What did it mean to Him? Somehow it revealed the truth of His being. Somehow it affirmed His identity by confirming Him to be the Beloved One in whom God's favour rested and rested so well. This relationship between Jesus and His God is more than we will ever know, more than servant, more than prophet, even more than Son.

It was Jesus' relationship with His God that fired and empowered His ministry. The transfiguration experience would have renewed Jesus' spirit and deepened His fervour in establishing the Kingdom of God.

As mentioned when we began this reflection, there is so much about Jesus and His life and ministry that we can never understand. But one thing is clearly evident in Jesus and in His mission: His capacity to surrender Himself to God. Such surrender can only be the fruit of a life-time of self-giving to the God of consummate love.

The soul is kissed by God in its innermost regions. With interior yearning, grace and blessing are bestowed. It is a yearning to take on God's gentle yoke, it is a yearning to give one's self to God's way. (2)

PART TWO: IMPLICATIONS

The implications for us concerning prayer and time alone are obvious. Anyone who is serious about their own personal growth and their ministry, knows that taking time out and spending it in prayer is not only enriching, it is imperative. What makes it imperative is what each one of us knows, in some way, deep in our being, and what Jesus knew so powerfully, that God is the centre and wellspring of our lives. " God is that in which the heart of a person rests." (3)

We know too that when we come to prayer, more often than not, we simply sit in long dry periods of silence. Yet even in that, something has happened for us; we have stopped. We have cleared a little space in our over hectic lives to simply be. We have given our spirits the opportunity to become more focused and more centred. If we are graced with even a hint of the awareness of God's Presence, as Jesus knew in His transfiguration experience, then we know how much prayer is God's gift to us and not something of our own doing.

Jesus' experience of prayer gives us the assurance that when we are burdened and weighed down or when we are overwhelmed and even in awe of what is happening in our lives and our ministry, we can find nourishment, renewed purpose, deeper conviction and direction by bringing it all to our God. Like Jesus, we are able to turn to God, not as we would go to someone to fix things, but as we would bring ourselves to fall into the comfort and support of one who loves us, ready to hear our ramblings and our ravings, ready to receive us just as we are for the sheer delight of being one with us.

Jesus' experience of prayer reminds us also that God is not the One "who waves magic wands" and removes all our difficulties and heartaches. Nor is God the one who "presses the button" that creates all our suffering! Hopefully there are times when we truly know what Jesus knew so well: that God is the one we come home to, the shoulder we cry on, the arms that embrace us and uphold us. God is the One, as Juliana of Norwich experienced, who wraps us up in love and encloses us in tenderness and in that tenderness never leaves us. (4)

The experience of prayer informs us better than any other source that when we do not nurture our spirits in this way we quickly lose balance, slip off-centre and out of focus. We become less sensitive to God's Presence in all our experiences. We find it difficult to see the big picture of God's reality in what happens. We fail to recognize God's movement in the events and circumstances of our daily lives. It is not that God is not present, it is that we have become insensitive, unaware, less vulnerable through a lack of familiarity, to the movement of God in our lives. Hence many sacred moments wash over us without our recognizing that we have been visited by God.

Surely it is a comfort for those to whom we relate and minister that we are people who are drawn to prayer. And people know if we are so inclined. Perhaps they recognize in us the markings of God's grace? Perhaps they see that we are not relying on our own resourcefulness but on the empowerment and inspiration of God? Perhaps they see a little more of God in our ministry and a little less of what is not of God in us?

While we may know the value of prayer in our lives, it doesn't make the struggle to find the time to pray any easier. For some, especially those with families, it can be extremely difficult to make time for prayer in the face of so many other demands. Having struggled to find the time, some are then pressured by the guilt of having taken time out from their other responsibilities.

Jesus would have known such pressures and difficulties. There were times when He and His disciples didn't even get time to eat (Mk 6:30–35). Yet it was His desire for God that enabled Him to find a way to take time alone in prayer.

"Marketplace" prayer, praying in the midst of our daily responsibilities and commitments, praying constantly, even in the midst of pressure and chaos, is really about being mindful; being quietly focused on God in all that we do. This may sustain us for a while and deepen our longing for time alone in prayer, but it will never satisfy the hunger of our soul. In time, that longing will cry out for our attention. Finding a way to take time out, if only briefly, can be the best remedy for our real hunger and longing.

Taking time out together, with those with whom we minister, can be for us what it was for Jesus and His disciples: the opportunity to simply be, to nurture our spirits, to reflect, to question and to pray. It may be for us the chance to ask the questions of our searching and share the faith of our journey and, in so doing, discover more fully the God of our believing. It may also be the most effective way to resource ourselves as a team for our ministry.

Essentially prayer, as we see it embodied in Jesus, is an invitation to fullness of life, to union with the God whose desire for us surpasses our deepest desire. The irony here is that fullness of life is not ours without the surrender of what we know to be life. And as we saw in Jesus' life, the more familiar we are with God's desire in our lives, then the more vulnerable we become to the movement of surrender.

Our rhythm here will not have the flow of familiarity that Jesus' had. We tend to resist rather than give over to the love that beckons us. Our ability to let go and allow surrender to *happen* in us will be the most substantial nourishment for our ministry. For out of this surrender new life will come in ways we would never imagine.

The more we give ourselves over to prayer the more susceptible we become to our own transfiguration, the experience wherein we are immersed in God so deeply that our being is affirmed, our image bears the likeness of God and our spirit is empowered to go forth.

Having said all that, the best way to appreciate the implications of prayer in our lives and our ministry is to simply give ourselves time alone, in quiet awareness of our God, and there, in the deep silence of our hearts, listen to the movement of God in our lives. For there we will recognize the true value of our being. We will know that we have in our midst One who is willing to receive the all and the nothingness of our spirit, ready to accept us as we are in that moment of being.

From the overflowing love of God there flows evermore into the soul a sweet, longing, hungry, love. (5)

That will be the love that claims us, frees us and sends us forth. Let us rest awhile in that love.

PART THREE: RESPONDING TO THE IMPLICATIONS

Personal Synthesis:

• You may prefer to take some time in quiet and prayer rather than deal with these questions.

1. What feelings do these reflections stir in you?

2. What issues and concerns do they raise for you?

3. What insights would you like to add to these reflections?

4. What aspect of Jesus' experience of prayer do you relate to in your life? In what way do you relate to this?

5. Find words or images that would express your own experience of prayer?

6. Does your experience of prayer impact in any way upon your ministry? If so, how does it effect your ministry? If not then why do you think it doesn't impact upon your ministry?

7. In what way have you known something of your own transfiguration, the experience of being immersed in God, the affirmation of your own being as the "Beloved" one of God? Remember that time now and simply be present to it in some way.

Scripture Reflection:

Spend some quiet time pondering the following text.

" Who do you say I am"? (Lk 9:18–20)

• Imagine yourself there in that space with Jesus praying alone in your company. How would you feel as you witnessed Him there? What do you sense is happening in Him? Why do you think He asked the question, "Who do people say I am"? What do you think He might have been thinking or feeling to provoke such a question?

• What would be your answer to Jesus' question? Do you have a sense of how those in your life perceive Jesus? Would you be surprised that Jesus asked your opinion about how others perceive Him? How would you respond to this question?

• Quieten your spirit and visualize the setting and atmosphere of this encounter. Imagine Jesus turning to you and asking, "But *you*, who do *you* say I am?" Listen! Imagine! Simply be!

For Group Sharing:

• Allow the group time to connect and gather before you begin discussing these questions. It is important to be aware of people's energy and readiness for what is to follow. In light of this, it may be more appropriate to be selective with these questions or even to disregard them and find another way for your group to respond to the implications.

1. Each share in some way with the group something of your own personal synthesis of these reflections.

2. What questions, concerns and issues do these reflections raise for you as a ministry team within your community?

3. Discuss when and how you pray together as a ministry team? What are the difficulties and obstacles here? What can you do as a team to nurture and develop a more genuine sharing of faith and prayer?

4. In what way would your community consider you to be people of prayer?

5. How does your prayer together impact upon your ministry and working relationships?

6. What initiatives could you develop that would enable your community to pray in some way with you as a team? What ini-

tiatives could you develop that would encourage and support people in your community in their efforts to share faith and prayer together?

RITUAL AND PRAYER

• The following are suggestions that may assist you in bringing your sharing to prayer. They are only suggestions and should not be considered in any other way. It would be better to create your own prayer and ritual than to rely on something that comes from outside your sharing.

Suggestions:

1. Create a sacred space and atmosphere of quiet and stillness within the group. Soften lights if necessary and play some quiet background music. Give people time to focus. Light a candle and place the Word and or relevant symbols within the centre of the group. Try to integrate into the sacred space something that has come from your sharing. Ensure that people are able to see the sacred focus, that they are comfortable and ready to enter into the prayerful spirit of this time.

2. Perhaps this time of prayer and ritual could be a very simple and gentle opportunity for personal meditation; time to centre one's self in the awareness of God.

Ensure that the space for this time is quiet and physically comfortable for people to rest within it. Invite people to spread out into their own space in the room and to relax their bodies and minds. Relaxation techniques and quiet music may be of help here.

Before you begin your meditation instruct the group about how long this time will be and inform them of the procedure to conclude the mediation. (Also discuss the plan of action for snoring so that it doesn't become a distraction for too long!)

3. The following scripture text could be used as a focus for the mediation. Have someone read it reflectively soon after the meditation begins.

    "This is my Beloved in whom I am well pleased" (Mt 17:5).

4. Some of the following songs may be of help at the beginning or end of the meditation (please refer to page 191 for location of songs):
    Sacred One (BUH)
    My Soul Is Longing (ARH)
    God of the Gentle Breeze (BUH)

5. Give people a little time to re-connect with the group and then share a meal or a drink or something that will enable people to celebrate and/or de-brief.

CHAPTER 6

CHALLENGE, FAILURE—EVEN DEATH

PART ONE: SCRIPTURAL REFLECTION

While Jesus' Presence was for so many sheer blessing from God, for others His Presence was challenging and threatening. There are many occasions reported in the gospels where the tension between Jesus and the religious leaders of His day was electric.

Jesus openly spoke out against the Scribes and Pharisees while they plotted and schemed in secret about how best to deal with Him. Jesus had their measure and knew exactly what He was dealing with (Mk 2:6–12), while they were continually baffled and confounded by Him. There was real conflict between Jesus and the Scribes and Pharisees. Jesus would call them "hypocrites, serpents, and brood of vipers" (Mt 23), while they in turn called Him "sinner, Satan and blasphemer" (Mt 26:65)! There is no question about it. Jesus rubbed the institution the wrong way!

We want to examine here why Jesus was such a challenge to the institutional religion of His day and what exactly did He challenge in the institution? Having identified that, we will consider the manner in which Jesus challenged the leaders and institution of His time.

In standing up to read from the scroll of the prophet Isaiah one Sabbath day, in the synagogue in His home town of Nazareth, Jesus proclaimed His mission as follows;

The spirit of the Lord has been given to me,
for he has anointed me.
He has sent me to bring the good news to the poor,
to proclaim liberty to captives
and to the blind new sight,
to set the downtrodden free,
to proclaim the Lord's year of favour (Lk 4:16–19).

It was Jesus' after-word that really exposed His purpose and His mission. As He rolled up the scroll He added, "This text is being fulfilled today even as you listen" (4:22).

As we discussed in chapter two, Jesus saw His mission as establishing the reign of God. It was not His intention to overthrow the institution nor undo the Law. Yet there was no possible way for Jesus to avoid conflict or challenge with the institution because, as outlined in His mission statement from Isaiah, it was to the poor, the captive, the blind and the downtrodden that the year of God's favour was to be proclaimed, not to the powerful, mighty or self-righteous.

Furthermore, in liberating the captives, Jesus exposed the captors. In giving new sight to the blind He identified those who refused to see. In setting the downtrodden free He unearthed the shackles and chains that weighed them down. And in proclaiming good news to the poor He revealed them to be blessed. In every area of His mission Jesus came up against the Scribes and Pharisees because they were the captors and the ones who refused to see. They were the ones burdening the downtrodden with practices and laws that oppressed them. They were the ones who judged the poor to be unworthy sinners.

Because Jesus was fired with a passion for the reign of God, He was inevitably forced by that passion to challenge the institution since, in so many ways, it contradicted the nature of God by its own values and practices (Mk 7:1–13).

In the face of the suffering and oppression of God's people, Jesus was compelled by love to lift them out of darkness into the light of God's Presence. Jesus was consumed by a single-hearted desire to do what God desired for God's people. And what God desired for God's people was life; life to the full (Jn 10:10). We recognise here in Jesus, His prophetic role in proclaiming the reign of God's Kingdom.

In honouring His heart's desire it seems that Jesus would directly and indirectly have to contend with the institution who perceived itself to be the exclusive mediators of God's salvation and the elite teachers of God's law. As with all the prophets that had gone before Him, Jesus, in remaining true to His mission, would undoubtedly come up against the establishment over His teaching and embodiment of God.

This is most evident in Luke's account of the healing of a crippled woman on the Sabbath (Lk 13:10–17). While Jesus is in the syna-gogue He notices a woman who for eighteen years had been crippled and bent over, unable, Luke reports, to stand upright (13:11).

Jesus calls to her and says, "Woman, you are rid of your infirmity" (13:12). He lays His hands on her and at once she straightens up and glorifies God. Now, while at the hands of Jesus, life is being renewed and what is bent over and twisted is being liberated, lifted up and healed, the officials are indignant.

It seems from their perspective of the law, healing and life and dignity cannot be attended to on the Lord's day but on any other day of the week! When the synagogue official concludes His proclamation of God's law, Jesus responds by calling him, "Hypocrite"! Jesus goes on to proclaim the law in terms of mercy and compassion and the officials, whom Mark calls Jesus' adversaries, are thrown into confusion (13:17).

In other similar encounters, such as the cure of the man with the withered hand (Mk 3:1–6), and the cure of the man born blind (Jn 9:1–41), Jesus' adversaries were not just thrown into confusion, they were furious and indignant, driven to destroy Him.

Jesus went about proclaiming and making real and immediate the God of life and liberation, while the Pharisees and Scribes were making the law their God. This is precisely why He was such a threat to them. It is the crux of what Jesus challenged in them: their perception and portrayal of God. The God of Jesus was unrecognizable to the Scribes and the Pharisees, they simply could not adjust their vision or enlighten their minds or open their stubborn hearts. While the blind were able to see the God of Jesus, the officials remained in darkness, unable to see (Jn 9:30–31).

In challenging their perception and image of God, Jesus in fact challenged not only their understanding and interpretation of the law but their values and moral code. Jesus exposed the religious elitism and manipulation of the Scribes and the Pharisees and was, as seen in Matthew's account of His indictment of them, unrelenting in the severity of His condemnation of them (Mt 23:1–39).

Jesus openly denounces the Scribes and the Pharisees and warns the people and His disciples to listen to them but not to do what they do because they do not practice what they preach. He names for the people, what they have been too afraid to name about their leaders; that they are hypocrites, self-serving power-brokers who parade around, flaunting their power while laying heavy burdens on people without ever attempting to ease the load of the oppressed.

Alas for them Jesus says, as He proceeds to unleash scathing remarks about their lack of integrity and justice, their corruption and lawlessness, their preoccupation with external incidentals and their neglect of what really matters.

His words are strong and passionate, His imagery of them full of anger and condemnation: "fools and blind guides, whitewashed tombs, serpents, brood of vipers!" And the term "hypocrites" which He repeats very often is the one that seems to pinpoint Jesus' anger the most, for they are as He says, appearing to be men of God when in fact they are not.

When the Pharisees and Scribes challenged Jesus about His disciples disregard for the tradition of the elders concerning the eating of food, Jesus quotes from the prophet Isaiah to them (Mk 7:1–13). He says,

It was of you hypocrites that Isaiah so rightly prophesied in this passage of scripture:

This people honours me with lip-service, while their hearts are far from me, the worship they offer me is worthless, the doctrines they teach are only human regulations (7:6–7).

This is the heart of Jesus' anger, that the Pharisees and Scribes have betrayed and dishonoured the God of their ancestors, the God whose love and mercy, compassion and justice has been denied the people by the religious hypocrisy and manipulation of these supposed leaders.

A classic example of the hypocrisy which Jesus exposed in the Scribes and Pharisees is the story of the Adulterous Woman from John's Gospel (Jn 8:2–11).

In typical Pharisee manner they present to Jesus someone who has broken the law, in this case a woman who was caught committing adultery. One could ask some interesting questions here about how she was actually "caught" in the act of committing adultery? It has overtones of watchdog-like behaviour by these keepers of the law who seem to be very anxious to have an open and shut case with which to catch Jesus out!

Jesus simply bends down and fingers the ground beneath Him, seemingly indifferent to their fervour in carrying out the law. In response to their persistent questioning of Him about His judgement of this woman, in view of Moses' law, He calmly says, "Let he who is without sin cast the first stone" (8:8). Here Jesus exposes their hypocrisy and their harsh judgement. One by one they slip away and Jesus is left alone with the woman.

Now we see the manner in which God's judgement is enacted. Jesus looks up at the woman. He does not stand over her but addresses her by inviting her to reflect on the situation. "Woman", He says, "where are they? Has no one condemned you?" (8:10).

Is Jesus helping the woman to see that even though she stands there alone with Him, exposed in her sin, she is not the only one caught in this drama of human brokenness and sin? Is He enabling her to see that in her vulnerable and exposed position, she in fact embodies the vulnerability and guilt of all of us? Is Jesus enabling her to see that no stones were thrown, no condemnation made because somehow Jesus turned the guilt of this woman around to be the guilt of all of us? We are reluctant to throw stones at ourselves!

The woman in her simple response to Jesus acknowledges that no one has condemned her. Finally, Jesus says to her, "Neither do I condemn you, go and sin no more." (8:11). His final gesture to this woman is forgiveness, so different from the outcome the Pharisees had planned for her.

We can see here that Jesus exposed and challenged not only the Pharisee's harsh embodiment of God's justice but also their hypocrisy in their application of the law.

It was not Jesus' intention to provoke or threaten the Scribes and Pharisees. His statement about His purpose being the fulfilment of the law and not its destruction, hints at one of the critical issues of contention between Jesus and the Scribes and Pharisees.

They were the ones who saw themselves as the *upholders* of the law, possessively guarding every letter of it. Jesus came and *interpreted* the law in terms of love and relationship with God and others, in terms of compassion and forgiveness, truth and freedom of spirit. Tony Kelly writes about Jesus' in this matter.

...In His fascinating presence, accepted values were radically reversed. Any religious law or tradition was made relative to the real love of God for struggling human beings. (1)

This was one of the fundamental differences between Jesus and the Scribes and Pharisees. From their perspective the law was to be obeyed, while for Jesus, the law was to be *fulfilled*. It was not just that their perspective of the law was different from Jesus' perspective. It was their ingenious ability to "get round the commandments of God in order to preserve their own tradition" (Mk 7:9), that was the real point of contention.

Jesus saw them for what they were: a law unto themselves and in that, they made "God's Word null and void" (7:13). This is the real "eye of the storm" in Jesus' heart concerning the Scribes and Pharisees: their abuse of God's Word, their failure to honour it and embody it as the religious leaders of God's people.

Jesus exposed them in this by embodying in His ministry, the true values of God's Kingdom. By His actions He embodied justice and mercy, forgiveness and compassion, and in so doing highlighted the religious corruption of these hypocritical leaders.

Jesus challenged them by focusing on God and the true worship of God rather than worship of the law. He declared that the Sabbath was made for man and woman, not man and woman for the Sabbath (Mk 2:27)!

He challenged them by speaking the truth and making them accountable to God. With Nicodemus, one of the leading Pharisees, who came to Him at night to seek out the truth, Jesus openly discusses the things of God with him. He explains that those who refuse to believe in the Son of God will be condemned by God; that even though the light has come into the world, some have shown that they prefer the dark (Jn 3:1–21).

Jesus challenged them, above all, by the authenticity and integrity of His Presence. This is evident when during a meal at Simon the Pharisee's house, a woman who "had a bad name in the town" came and washed Jesus' feet with her tears and dried them with her hair (Lk 7:36–50). Jesus responded to this woman with respect and acceptance. Simon, Jesus' host, judged it to be an inappropriate response to the woman, given that she was a sinner.

Jesus did not respond as the Pharisees expected Him to, not in this case or in any other situation. On the contrary, He accepted the expression of love from this woman whom the Pharisees judged to be a sinner. While they judged her Jesus loved her, forgave her many sins and affirmed her dignity.

Jesus challenged the institutional leaders by remaining faithful to His heart's desire: the establishment of the reign of God. In so doing He enfleshed and made real a new experience of God. The God that Jesus embodied was for the Scribes and the Pharisees the greatest threat to the idolatrous gods they had created for themselves. This threat was so challenging because the God of Jesus was validated by the liberation and affirmation of the poor and oppressed, to be the God of their ancestors, the living and true God.

Jesus, in His ministry, had in essence freed and dissociated the living and true God from the captivity of the Scribes and Pharisee's religious manipulation. In so doing Jesus gave all who were broken and outcast, all who were sinners and in need, all who were humble of heart and poor in spirit, the opportunity the religious leadership of the Scribes and Pharisees had denied them. He gave them the opportunity to come into the transforming grace of God's Presence; to be welcomed, healed and blessed by God.

When John the Baptist's disciples come to Jesus on behalf of John and asked, "Are you the One who is to come or must we wait for another?" Jesus presents the criteria for assessing the validity of who He was and what He did,

Go back and tell John what you have seen and heard. The blind see again, the lame walk, lepers are cleansed, and the deaf hear, the dead are raised to life and the Good News is proclaimed to the poor (Lk 7:18–23).

What an extraordinary resume! What a remarkable measure of the authenticity of one's being and one's ministry—the healing, liberating and affirmation of others!

Jesus goes on to note that the one who does not lose faith in Him will be happy (7:23). He acknowledges the lack of faith in His contemporaries, the Scribes and the Pharisees and says that by their refusal to accept God's plan they had thwarted what God had in mind for them (Lk 7:28–34).

And thwart it they did! The glorious season of Jesus' springtime in the desert of people's lives was shattered by the darkest and the most deadly wintertime. Jesus was taken away from those who had come not only to love Him, but had come to live in the light of His Presence. It was as though God had been snatched from them and, with that, all that they had come to find life and hope in had turned to darkness. Jesus, it seemed, had failed them. The promise that He had made that the Kingdom would be theirs, and all the new teaching He had proclaimed, it all seemed to be folly now as Jesus was led away to be crucified.

Jesus had warned them that suffering would come and that darkness would overtake them (Mk 9:30–32). But in the flourishing life of springtime, any talk of wintery nights was too readily dismissed. All through His arrest and His torture, even as he carried His cross to Calvary and right to the moment of His death, many of them would have been hoping that this nightmare would turn around. No doubt they would have grappled with the thought that if Jesus truly was who they had come to believe He was, then surely He would not really die. Surely death would not be the last word of One who embodied life so fully?

And when Jesus breathed His last breath and gave up His spirit, the darkest void they had ever known descended upon them. For now they were left with nothing but death and the unbearable thought that Jesus had failed. The movement had collapsed and now lay in a shattered mess at the foot of Jesus' cross. He had failed to overthrow the corrupt institution from which He was enabling them to break free. He had failed to liberate them from their poverty and the oppression of the Romans. In fact, for many of them, Jesus had died without changing anything of their daily reality, without changing anything except the sense of God they had tasted in Him.

But even that, their only remaining sign of what He had achieved, was so fragile now, so plagued by doubt and confusion it was of little, if any, consolation to them. When Jesus died it seemed to them God had died with Him, at least the God they had come to delight in. And this was the ultimate pain for them. It was not just their grief and loss of Jesus that pained them, it was that they felt there was no God for them without Jesus. Having experienced the God of Jesus how could they possibly be satisfied with the God of the institution, how could they go back to what they knew before

Jesus? The only God that was truly believable to them it seems had gone with Jesus. Sebastian Moore says of their experience,

Those dark days would be much more radical desolation than what we call Dark Night of the Soul. The person who enters the Dark Night does not look back on such a heaven-on-earth as did the followers of Jesus. For them, God had involved himself so much in the life and the movement of Jesus that the failure of the movement was much more like the death of God than His mere absence. (2)

To those without the eyes of faith, Jesus certainly did fail. He was beaten down and destroyed by the institution. They had won it seems! But for those with the eyes to see and the hearts to know, there is a conviction, a conviction of faith that enables one to see that in the darkest death, the seed of life germinates in the tomb experience of desolation and nothingness, of void and stone cold lifelessness. For those with the eyes of faith, failure and death are not what they appear to be!

PART TWO: IMPLICATIONS

W hat are the implications of all this for us? Does the fact that Jesus challenged the leadership and institution of His day give us an excuse to do the same in our day? That is certainly not the point here. It is not so much that Jesus challenged and appeared to be anti-establishment to the religious leaders of His day that is of interest to us here. It is the prophetic nature of Jesus that is of real importance to us: *why* Jesus challenged, *what* He challenged and *how* He challenged? It is the implications of these questions in our own lives and in our ministry that we wish to consider here.

1. WHY CHALLENGE?

The validity of any challenge is its motivation. And the motivation that validates any challenge we may feel needs to be addressed in our faith communities, is the motivation that Jesus had: to honour the reign of God and God's values. This motivation is what identifies a genuine prophet from a person who is antagonistic and merely anti-establishment.

Being a prophet is not something one chooses, but something that one is compelled to embrace. It is a call and an invitation initiated by God that cannot be refused. It is a call and invitation that pursues one's soul unrelentingly.

Prophets then, are individuals or groups of people who are called both to listen and to speak out. They must listen to God, to the 'signs of the times' and to the cries of the oppressed and when they have understood the message, speak out, whatever the personal cost. Prophets are no holier than anyone else. They are frequently very wounded people—but like Jeremiah or Isaiah, they put their woundedness at the service of God. When they hear the voice which says 'Whom shall I send? Who will be our messenger?' to their horror, they find themselves answering, 'Here I am, send me' (3).

Anyone who is foolish enough in the eyes of the world to be prophetic, to speak the truth and challenge injustice needs to have a sure base and good measure of what they are about. The measure is, as we saw in Jesus' life and ministry, God's way. Anything that is not of God or thwarts the way of God is liable to question and challenge by those who are serious in their commitment to honour the reign of God.

If we are fired with a passion for God's Kingdom then we will be people who at times, are in conflict with any group or leadership in our communities that are pharisaical in their values, attitudes and practices.

This will demand of us honest self-searching and discernment before God. The prophet who speaks the truth and calls to accountability those who are thwarting God's way is one who stays close to the heart and mind of God, fully focused on the way of God.

This means that we need to be aware of our own agenda and painfully, in many cases, lay aside our own needs or views and speak on behalf of those who have no voice, just as Jesus did for the poor and oppressed in His community. Essentially, challenging as Jesus did means that we need to be prepared to walk the path that Jesus walked, the path of rejection and judgement, the path of accusations and misunderstanding. To walk the path of Jesus is to experience, at times, apparent failure and even crucifixion. It is to live in the experience of the dark tomb, waiting, hoping in lifelessness for the resurrection that some might consider never comes.

It is the reality of walking this path that deters so many from their prophetic role of speaking the truth in honour of God's Kingdom. We will consider this more deeply further on in our discussions.

For now let us examine some of the things we need to challenge in our own communities.

2. WHAT NEEDS TO BE CHALLENGED?

If Jesus were to walk our streets where would He feel most at home and welcomed? Would He stand in our communities or would He sit in the gutters of our society with those who are outside our Churches? Would He stand with the politically correct, the power-brokers of our Church or would He kneel with the real pillars of our communities, the simple, loyal hardworking folk? Who would Jesus embrace as kindred spirit? Who would He affirm? Who would He invite to His table?

What we are really asking here is what and whom would Jesus challenge in our Church and society today? We need to ask that question because if we are serious about following Jesus then we need to challenge what He would challenge in our contemporary Church and society?

a) We challenge whatever is not of God

We know if something is of God by the fruit it bears. We saw earlier that Jesus validated His mission as the One sent by God by noting that the blind see, the deaf hear, the lame walk, the lepers are cleansed, the dead are raised to new life and the Good News is proclaimed to the poor (Lk 7:18–23).

Whatever contradicts or thwarts this transforming grace of God is what we need to challenge in both our faith communities and our wider communities. Whatever attitudes, practices and policies keep people in the dark unable to see, prevent them from hearing, prohibit and limit their freedom and dignity, is what needs to be challenged. Whatever isolates people in their brokenness and shame, restricts or hinders the life in them and disclaims the blessedness and dignity of their spirits is what needs to be challenged. Whatever and however injustices are experienced, this is the agenda for justification and challenge.

As mentioned in chapter two, the policies, values, attitudes and initiatives that contradict the nature of the God we proclaim are the things we need to challenge. Whatever practice or attitude or value in our community creates a sense of inconsistency, discrepancy, hypocrisy and injustice in light of the God of Jesus, is our agenda for challenge and change.

b) We challenge religious manipulation, elitism and power

Jesus made it very clear in His indictment of the religious leaders of His day that any show of power and domination of God's people by them will be judged harshly by God. What are the signs of elitism, power and domination in our communities? How authentic is the spiritual and pastoral leadership in our communities?

Note here the word is *authentic* not *perfect*. We are not on about challenging what is genuine human struggle but only what is not of God. Power and elitism in any form contradicts the equality and mutuality of God's love. When such contrary attitudes denigrate and disempower individuals or groups in our community then we are compelled by our commitment to the dignity of all to speak out against it.

Leadership that is closed and preoccupied with power creates fear and forces issues to be hidden rather than brought out into the light of day. This in turn creates a smouldering of discontent, murmuring and anger. Gradually, basic values of justice and charity are overlooked or neglected. People become disempowered and unable or unwilling to contribute to the life of the community. In some cases they only stay, out of necessity rather than out of commitment.

Any leadership that forces, by its domination, matters of charity and justice to be left unaddressed, is a leadership that is thwarting the building up of God's Kingdom. That leadership needs to be made accountable to the community before God.

So too any form of religious manipulation in our communities needs to be exposed and addressed. Religious manipulation comes in many forms. Often it is disguised as a liturgical norm, or canon law, or theological principle while all the time it is about the personal preference or personal perspective of the particular pastor or leader.

What would Jesus have to say to some of our pastors and leaders who, for example, deny their communities *basic liturgical rights* as the people of God or *spiritual renewal*, because they as pastor or leader do not like or do not feel comfortable with what is proposed. To mis-name the particular issue as being "liturgically incorrect" or "not in keeping with Church teaching", rather than owning it as one's personal struggle or one's disapproval of the particular matter, is dishonest and deceptive. More than that, it does not allow for or promote better interpersonal understanding, openness and growth. Often this kind of manipulation is exposed in absolute statements such as "not in *my* Church!" Jesus would very quickly ask , "Whose Church?"

Leadership that does not liberate, that keeps people spiritually captive, that burdens the community with attitudes and values that keep them downtrodden and contradicts the God of Jesus in its practices and policies, is leadership that needs to be challenged and made accountable. How we challenge and call people into accountability is just as critical as why we do it.

3. HOW DO WE CHALLENGE?

a) In the way of Jesus

We do what Jesus did. We discern what our deepest heart's desire is. If it is to honour God's reign in our own lives and the lives of those with whom we minister, then we are compelled to speak the truth. But first we must wrestle with and own in our hearts what is of God and what is not of God, putting aside as best we can whatever would prevent us from speaking God's truth.

Often this is the hardest step, sorting out what is God's agenda and what is our own. This is so delicate because we get tangled up and pulled off-centre, away from our focus by our emotions, usually our very justifiable anger or frustration. Perhaps we need to wait in that space until we have calmed our spirits and are clear enough to hear God's wisdom and truth, so that what is of God becomes the base from which we move to address the issue.

If we challenge in honour of God's reign, then we will try to do it more by our actions than by our words, more by the authenticity and integrity of our presence. We will do our best to get on with the matter at hand, trying to embody in our lives what is of God, relating to others out of the values of God. The measure of our authenticity and integrity here will be in what we do and how we respond when we fail in our efforts to challenge. If we harbour resentment, or promote destructive undercurrents or provoke con- frontation, we will surely be working against genuine reconcilia- tion and change.

Nurturing as genuinely as one can, a spirit of respect and a desire to befriend those involved, can be an effective way to approach a situation of challenge. Jesus often accepted dinner invitations from Pharisees and in accepting their hospitality was able to connect with them (Lk 7:36–50). Acknowledging who they are and where they are; trying to see issues from their perspective, to step into their shoes and stand within their territory; letting them know that you understand and respect their position and perspective, can oftentimes be a more beneficial way to challenge. Applying the finer sensitivities of mediation rather than confrontation may help to disarm potentially explosive situations.

Being prepared to let oneself be challenged too can promote better dialogue and mutual exchange. Taking a defensive or aggressive stance usually delivers only what it gives, more defensiveness and aggression. Being open and willing to hear the other side of the situation or matter can immediately disengage defensiveness in the other. Trying to build up a sense of mutual respect and concern rather than judgemental and sometimes holier-than-thou attitudes may require much harder work from us but, in the end, may bring about the better outcome.

Keeping the issues out there, up front and the centre of attention rather than personal attacks usually indicates that one is focused and not just being hot-headed about the issue. In the heat of the moment this is very difficult. But even when tempers have been lost and the edges more than frazzled, the ability to own one's part, to apologize and begin again is in itself the way of God.

b) A united voice

One of the most common reasons why situations of injustice go unchecked in our communities is the fear of reprisal. Teachers, for example, fear they will lose their job if they challenge their leadership. Their leadership in turn feel they will lose their jobs if they challenge their directors and bishops. Parish members fear they will be black marked or even alienated from the community should they raise issues with some of their pastors. And some of our best pastors are suppressed and kept down by bishops who refuse to hear them or address their issues of concern. So the cycle of disempowerment goes on in organizations when people harden their hearts and block their ears.

This cycle of disempowerment will continue until such leadership is made accountable to those whom they are supposedly serving. One voice is less likely to be heard and more easily dismissed. But many voices united as one, many people standing as one are far more difficult to block out and dismiss. It is highly unlikely that a whole staff would be dismissed or that a whole leadership team disengaged, or a whole community isolated.

The problem here is achieving a genuine united effort. People usually prefer one voice to speak on their behalf while the others stand back at a safe and anonymous distance. Another difficulty here is that the motivation and commitment level of people vary so much that it is difficult to maintain a clear, genuine motive for the group's action.

I am convinced that in some situations, if there were a united effort in bringing our leadership to accountability, change would eventually come about. I am not advocating revolution or mutiny-type activity. I am, however, suggesting that serious discernment and genuine acceptance of our responsibility as followers of Jesus would see more voices unite and more of what is not of God challenged and made accountable.

4. THE FAILURE OF IT ALL

In the final analysis, all of this can fail, and sadly, in some cases does fail. Idealizing and theorizing about how to approach leadership or anyone with whom we experience conflict is often far removed from the reality. The fact is, no matter how well we handle confrontation in this arena, as with the case of Jesus, our voices will often fall on deaf ears, our perspective will remain unseeable to blinded eyes and our concerns unheeded by stubborn closed hearts. As with Jesus the situation may never change.

What do we do when in spite of our sincere efforts, our risk-taking and sacrifices, nothing comes of it except heartache for us? It is hard not to become bitter and resentful. Somehow holding on to the conviction that there is a bigger picture which in time will reveal itself, may be all we can do.

Realizing that miracles may not have happened, circumstances may not have changed, external realities of injustice may remain the same and worse still, those in question may even have gained more power, can be utterly discouraging and debilitating.

It is hard to see that there might be miracles of a different sort hidden in places we can barely observe. Perhaps the miracles are in the shifting within the heart or in a change of attitude, or other such less noticeable transformations. Jesus' life and death shows us that nothing in the cause of God is ever wasted. The problem is having the perception of God to notice what really has been gained.

Knowing when to let go, when to surrender into the utter darkness as Jesus did, without any certainties of what will become of all that we struggled with and for, takes enormous faith. Trusting that good will come from our efforts even in ways we could never imagine is also about a special kind of faith. It is the same faith that every prophet has had to grapple with, even to the point of death.

It is only the foolish wisdom of the cross, the paradox of life hidden in the buried seed, that makes any sense out of what we struggle with in all this. The deep conviction that in time, through the darkest night, gradually a new and glorious dawn will rise within our spirits, may be at times all that we have for life!

Let us now apply the relevance of all this to our immediate reality.

PART THREE: RESPONDING TO THE IMPLICATIONS

Personal Synthesis:

1. What feelings do these reflections stir in you?

2. What issues and concerns do they raise for you?

3. What insights would you like to add to these reflections?

4. What has been and what is your own personal experience concerning the implications presented here? Are you one who has been or is being challenged? Are you the one who has been challenging or still is challenging?

    What have you learnt about yourself in this area?

5. What defences do you employ when you are being challenged? What strengths do you have that enable mediation to happen?

6. What are the issues and concerns that urge you to speak out the truth in situations you are involved in? What can you do in such situations? What prevents you from taking a stand or speaking your truth? What are the steps along the way to resolution that you could take?

Scripture Reflection:

Take some quiet time to reflect upon the following text.

Jesus before the Sanhedrin (Mt 26:57–68)

• What sense do you have of Jesus in this situation? Is there a particular aspect of this situation that provokes some kind of emotion in you? What is the situation and what does it cause you to feel?

• When have you experienced judgement and condemnation? When have you felt ridiculed and unjustly treated? How have you responded to that treatment?

• Does the experience of Jesus' condemnation and apparent failure offer you any comfort or insight? How does His experience impact upon your own experience in this area of your life?

• What would you say to Jesus if you were standing beside Him in front of that Sanhedrin? What would Jesus say to you if He were to stand beside you in front of your place of judgement and condemnation? What do you need to sustain you in your truth?

For Group Sharing:

• Allow the group time to connect and gather before you begin discussing these questions. It is important to be aware of people's energy and readiness for what is to follow. In light of this, it may be more appropriate to be selective with these questions or even to disregard them and find another way for your group to respond to the implications.

1. Each share in some way with the group something of your own personal synthesis of these reflections.

2. What questions, concerns and issues do these reflections raise for you as a ministry team within your community?

3. Who are the Christ-like prophets in your community? What is their challenge to you and your community? How do you respond to them? What enables you to be open to them? What prevents you from meeting them? What steps can you initiate toward an opportunity to dialogue with them?

4. In light of the values of God's Kingdom, who or what needs to be called to accountability in your immediate community and in your wider community? What are the matters and concerns that cause you as a team to question and challenge a particular situation? What positive steps could you take toward genuine dialogue?

5. How open and approachable are you as a team, in this area of challenge and accountability? What can you do to become

more open and receptive to the insight and feedback of others?

6. What are the conflicts and tensions within your own team that need to be addressed? What positive steps can you each take toward a process that may enable these matters to be addressed? How can you reconcile your differences, forgive the wrongs and let go of your grievances? How can you grow through what appears to be failure?

7. Take some quiet time and reflect upon your sharing. Find a word or phrase that would express to the group one thing you have learnt about yourself in this and one thing you have learnt about others.

RITUAL AND PRAYER

* The following are suggestions that may assist you in bringing your sharing to prayer. They are only suggestions and should not be considered in any other way. It would be better to create your own prayer and ritual than to rely on something that comes from outside your sharing.

Suggestions:

1. Create a sacred space and atmosphere of quiet and stillness within the group. Soften lights if necessary and play some quiet background music. Give people time to focus. Light a candle and place the Word and or relevant symbols within the centre of the group. Try to integrate into the sacred space something that has come from your sharing. Ensure that people are able to see the sacred focus, that they are comfortable and ready to enter into the prayerful spirit of this time.

2. Prepare a simple reconciliation ritual for this session.Give people the opportunity through silence and reflection to own their failure, their grievances, their brokenness and sin and to

ritualize in some way the surrender of this to God. Again symbols and rituals such as incense, burning, water and blessing could be helpful in this.

Provide an opportunity for the team to own and articulate how it has failed to be open to the community and the challenge that may be coming from the community or individuals within the community. Ritualize this in some way that will enable the team to move forward and outward.

3. The following scripture may be appropriate.
    Mt 7:1–5
    Mt 5:23–26; 39–48
    I've come to cast a fire...
    1 Th:4:12–18

4. Some of the following songs may be helpful (please refer to page 191 for location of songs):
    Gather Us (ARH)
    O My Strength (BUH)
    My Plans for You (GOL)
    To Whom Shall We Go (BUH)
    I Cry To You (ARH)
    Are You With Me Lord? (GOL)
    A New Dawn (BUH)

5. At the conclusion of your prayer, share a meal or a drink or something that will enable people to celebrate and/or de-brief.

CHAPTER 7

EMMAUS JOURNEY—FROM DEATH TO LIFE

PART ONE: SCRIPTURAL REFLECTION

What was Jesus' last word? Was it about death or was it about life? As we saw in our previous chapter, for those who had come to believe in Jesus, His death was a devastation, not just through the loss of Jesus, but for them it was a sense of having lost the truest experience of God they had known.

So we find two of them journeying away from the place of their deepest despair, Jerusalem, that holy city whose streets were now filled with the cries of all those who ached for Jesus and whose darkened dwellings now hid them as they clung together in their grief and fear.

What had happened to the believers? What were they thinking? What were they feeling about all that had happened? What had been glorious light for them in the company of Jesus was now, in His absence, a darkness that weighed heavily upon their spirits. So they journey away from Jerusalem, that place of darkness and death, on the road to Emmaus.

Let us journey with them on this Emmaus way. Let us take time now to ponder their questions and search out their meaning.

As they journey, they talk and reflect on all that they had experienced. What would their questions have been? What explanations were they trying to console themselves with? How were they making sense of what was seemingly a senseless death? For what meanings were they searching? How would they continue without Him?

They journey on, their spirits burdened and downcast. What was their deepest concern as they walked and talked? Were they angry with Jesus? Had they seen a way to avoid this failure and death? Why hadn't He listened to them? Why did He insist on returning to Jerusalem? Why had He been so foolish, so trusting, so outspoken? Did they doubt what Jesus had said and done?

As the journey continues so does their questioning. What if all they thought they knew about Jesus was not real? What if Jesus had been what the Pharisees had judged Him to be? If He were the great prophet they believed Him to be then why did God let Him die? What wrong had He done, what harm had He caused? Did they understand who Jesus really was?

As they journey further, they grapple with their confusion. What had happened to His body? Had He really died? What if someone had taken it? What had He said about rising? How could it possibly happen? Did they believe in Jesus?

And into their midst on this journey comes one who appears as stranger to them. Did they sense something familiar about Him?

How did He know that their spirits were sad? What was it about Him that was eluding them as He walked by their side?

What did they think of this stranger as He asked what they were talking about? Why didn't He know what had happened when everyone else in Jerusalem knew? Perhaps it was something in His eyes that left them wondering about Him. Or perhaps it was the way He listened to them and their story.

And there was something in the way He responded to their story. How did He understand so much? How had He come to know so much about Jesus? And what was it about the way He explained things to them? How was He able to make so much sense of it all? And what was that feeling burning in their hearts as they listened to Him?

When they drew near to Emmaus how did they feel when He made as if to go on? What was it about this stranger that left them wanting more of Him? Why did they press Him to stay with them?

What did they feel as they sat at table with Him? Did it awaken a memory in them? And when He took the bread in His hands what did they sense in Him? When He blessed and broke it and gave it to them what did they recognize in Him? Did they realize that there was only One who could take bread in His hands like that? Did they feel again in the way that He broke the bread the Presence they had known only with Jesus? Was it in His hands, His eyes? Was it in His Presence? And as their eyes were opened what did they know in their hearts?

Could the One for whom they grieved and longed be with them now? But how? How could this be? They had seen Him die. They knew it was real death for they had felt the utter desolation of His absence. And now, now there was a deep burning in their hearts. Now in their midst, there was a Presence amongst them, one that they recognized. How could this be? Was the struggle with death now a mystery of life?

Jesus had met them on their journey right in the midst of their despair. He had noticed their spirits and had invited them to share their story. In response to their story He shared His own Christ story. In doing so Jesus made sense of their story. Where they were without meaning and understanding, Jesus, by His own story, had given them new meaning. Where they were without hope Jesus had, by His story, given them a new and deeper hope. Jesus had made sense of all that they struggled with.

No wonder they wanted more of Him. In accepting their hospitality, at table with them, in communion with them, Jesus revealed Himself to them as living Presence (Lk 24:13–35).

So real was His Presence to them, so deeply had it burned within them that they immediately went back to the place of their pain and dread. They returned to Jerusalem with new hearts.

For these disciples, and for those who shared with them their story of Jesus, death was in no way the last word of Jesus. The experience of God they thought they had lost in the death of Jesus was, once again, yet in a new way, accessible to them. There was no doubt in their hearts that Jesus had risen. For He had impassioned them again, fired their hearts and empowered them to return to the place of death to proclaim a story of life!

There was a Presence amongst them now, a Presence that only the truest faith could know. So sacred was this Presence, so powerfully real that their fear gave way to a peace and a joy that they had never known, to an understanding and conviction that fired them with the courage to proclaim Jesus as living Presence within us!

Utter madness! Ultimate deception! No denouncement of madness or deception could quell what they knew in the core of their being—the Spirit of Jesus was within them in a way that no heady rationalization could comprehend; within them in a way that only a graced heart could embrace.

The resurrection of Jesus allowed the disciples and believers to claim within themselves the Spirit they had always sensed in Jesus but had not comprehended.

The Spirit that had stirred in their hearts when Jesus had walked amongst them and had spoken to them, was the Spirit they were now able to embrace. It was the same Spirit that had always been there in Jesus when He touched them and healed them. It was the same Spirit there in Jesus when He forgave them and affirmed them, when He laughed and cried with them. The Spirit they sensed in Him then was the Spirit within them now.

And this Spirit had given to them all that Jesus had promised it would give: an understanding of what Jesus had done, a living memory of all that had been, a conviction of who Jesus was. Fullness of life was possible for them now, not simply in remembering what Jesus had said and done, but in allowing the Spirit of Jesus to live and breathe within them. Jesus' last word was most surely for them, not about death but about true life!

PART TWO: IMPLICATIONS

The Emmaus journey is a magnificent account of resurrection, not just in Jesus, but resurrection in the hearts of those who journeyed from darkness and death to light and new life because of Jesus' Presence. Let us consider here some of the implications of this journey in our own lives.

1. CRUCIFIXION—DECLARATION OF LOVE

Before we can appreciate the glory of resurrection we need to face the darkness of crucifixion.

The crucifixion of Jesus at the hands of a humanity blinded to God's loving Presence in their midst, is God's ultimate declaration of unconditional love for us. In the crucifixion and death of Jesus, God meets our humanity at the deepest level of our evil, at the very core of our most defiant and convincing rejection of God, in the face of God's most vulnerable and most total self-giving. Sebastian Moore reflects on this when, in discussing the way to God he says,

...it consists in becoming convinced of God's love as an all-penetrating force: then coming to experience evil in myself as a reality so pervasive and elusive as to its origin, that I cannot experience it as accepted by God in love without the presence of some other factor in which God's love would go to meet my evil. This other factor is the crucifixion and death of Jesus when this is regarded precisely as 'authorized' by God to declare God's love for us. For in this conception, God obeys the deepest psychological law of acceptance: to be convinced of my acceptance, I must know that I am accepted at my worst. (1)

In Ezekiel 16 we get a glimpse of the God who meets us at our worst, in our raw, naked humanity. Let us see here what God does with us at the point of our deepest vulnerability.

I saw you struggling in your blood as I was passing....the very day you were born there was no-one to cut your naval-string, or wash you in cleansing water, or rub you with salt or wrap you in napkins...you were exposed; you were as unloved as that on the day you were born... I bathed you in water, I washed the blood from you, I anointed you with oil...You developed, you grew, you reached marriageable age. Your breasts and your hair both grew but you were quite naked...I spread part of my cloak over you and covered your nakedness...I gave you embroidered dresses...I put a beautiful diadem on your head...You grew more and more beautiful. The fame of your beauty spread throughout the nations, since it was perfect because I had clothed you with my own splendour... (Ez 16:4–14).

The crucifixion confirms that God knows the full extent of our bloodied nakedness and not only meets us in it but perceives beauty in us. What kind of knowing is this; what kind of perception of our humanity does God have? This is a knowing and acceptance that only the One who is love itself is capable of. It is an acceptance and love able to transform even bloodied mess!

Here we see that more than meet us and accept us at our worst, God forgives and restores a loving relationship with us, not in the sense that God begins to love us again having withheld that love until we own our sin. No, the sense of restoring a loving relationship here is the sense of the faithful Lover whose love is so steadfast, so unconditional that it waits and waits with longing, always believing in and hoping for the homecoming of the beloved.

But the waiting of this God of faithful love is not passive, nor is it, on the other hand, intrusive of our freedom to respond. The waiting of God as we struggle to come home is in the spirit of the Lover who lures us to desert places and there, where we are most vulnerable, speaks to our hearts of a love that is so intimate that it can be refused no longer (Hosea 2:16).

What does all this tell us? That we are known by God at the core of our being, in that endless chasm where good and bad, life and death, God and human being interact within us. Not only are we known by God but we are accepted unconditionally in love, seen as important enough, worthy enough to be graced with God's own Presence.

We matter to God more than we matter to ourselves because in us God's Spirit claims our spirit as God's own Spirit, our image as God's own image and our likeness of being as God's own likeness. God sees in us what we cannot see in ourselves. God sees a reflection of God's own self in us (2 Cor 3:18). God's self-loving is so selfless that it gives birth to God's Spirit in us, a complete and utter overflowing of authentic divine love. Once again Sebastian Moore enlightens us.

Is not this central affair we have with the ultimate mystery the thing which gives shape to all our relationships? The reason why I feel a growth in my worth when I know I am significant to a significant other is that I am psychically wedded, of my very nature, to the significant other that gives me my being. (2)

This is why God speaks of seeing us as precious, as being reverenced and honoured by God. This is why God promises to meet us and save us in the midst of our human struggle, to call us by name and lead us through the deep waters and fires that may engulf us (Is 43:1–7).

The crucifixion of Jesus is God's pledge of honour and reverence of our worth, God's declaration of unconditional love for us.

2. A RESURRECTION PERSPECTIVE

With the new and glorious dawn of resurrection, the disciples experienced the growing enlightenment of who Jesus really was, a gradual understanding of what the something more they had experienced in Jesus was really about. The resurrection not only made sense of what Jesus said and did but, more importantly, it made absurd sense of who Jesus really was—truly God and, in a most authentic way, truly human.

This is the ultimate paradox, not so surprisingly life from death, but remarkably God as human being amongst us. The implication here is not just about life coming from death but it is about *how* that life comes, in One who lived and died *as one of us*.

The resurrection of Jesus affirms forever the transcendent capacity of the human spirit. "From His fullness we have all received grace upon grace" (Jn 1:16). When the human spirit opens itself and embraces the God within, resurrection happens as a new dawn in the heart of the human spirit, wherein hope overcomes despair, light shines in darkness and life rises forth from death.

Just as the resurrection enabled the disciples on the road to Emmaus to appreciate what was at the heart of Jesus' life and thus make sense of their own experience, so too the resurrection enables us to make sense of our human reality (Lk 24:13–35).

In the grip of darkness and struggle it is nearly impossible to see the light and find the meaning. Often it is in retrospect that we realize that hope has deepened, courage has strengthened, life has been renewed, good has come from what first seemed to be destruction. We come to a fuller understanding of what life is about and what really matters when we view it from a resurrection perspective.

Without the resurrection what we live and struggle with is futile and meaningless. Resurrection reminds us of the big picture, of the something more. It enables us to live with a new vision, a new perspective and a sure hope. Resurrection enables us to live with paradoxes as Jesus did.

Jesus' life, death and resurrection validates the Christian's "foolish wisdom" (1Cor 1:18–31). It is a wisdom that knows by its lived experience that authenticity is birthed in suffering, that there is wholeness in brokenness, there is strength in weakness and ful-filment in surrender. It is this "foolish wisdom" that refines our spirits, as gold in fire (Prov 27:21), enabling the fullness of God's life to flourish in us.

3. SPIRIT—SHEKINAH PRESENCE

To believe in the resurrection of Jesus is to believe that from the fullness of Jesus' life, death and resurrection, we have received grace upon grace (Jn 1:16). The meaning implicit here is that the same Spirit that glorified Jesus has been poured into our hearts (Rom 8:11).

This outpouring of the Spirit of Jesus is perhaps the most intimate self-giving of God. To help us appreciate this I would like to refer to our Jewish inheritance.

In Hebrew Rabbinic writings, the feminine noun "Shekinah", derived from the Hebrew word "Shakkan" meaning "to dwell", was used to refer to God's indwelling. Specifically it was used in reference to God's Presence in the temple. More widely in Rabbinic tradition it referred in a special way to God's indwelling amongst God's people. It has been used within that tradition and still is today, as the reverential name for God's nearness to God's people. (3)

The Presence of God which Shekinah suggests is not only God's active, alluring Presence, but more especially, God's intimate Presence amongst God's people. In our Christian tradition God's Presence amongst us is referred to as the Holy Spirit. It is impor-tant to note that reference to the Holy Spirit, the Spirit that Jesus promised would inflame the hearts of the disciples, is repeatedly used after the resurrection of Jesus. There is no doubt that the dis-ciples knew this Spirit as the living Presence of Jesus (Rom 8:9; Gal 4:6).

In the light of our Christian tradition we can glean further riches from this beautiful Jewish sense of God's Presence, when we consider the notion of Shekinah as God's indwelling in the temple in reference to our Christian tradition of temple: "Did you not know that you are the Temple of God" (1 Cor 3:16–17)? In this context the meaning is explicit: God's intimate Presence dwells within the core of our being. Shekinah rests within us.

As in the Jewish tradition, when Shekinah journeyed with the people during their suffering and oppression, their displacement and homelessness, intimately one with them in all their desert wanderings, so too the Spirit of Jesus remains with us in our daily struggles and desert wanderings. Elizabeth Johnson expresses it beautifully.

Shekinah...signifies no mere feminine dimension of God but God as She-Who-Dwells-Within, divine presence in compassionate engagement with the conflictual world, source of vitality and consolation in the struggle. (4)

Jesus' promise never to abandon us is faithfully honoured in the Spirit who dwells within us. It is that Spirit who is God's own Spirit, God's deepest self, searching not only the depths of our human spirit, but searching even God's own depth. This is the Spirit who has been poured into our hearts as gift, that we may know the things of God, that we may have words to cry out to God, that we may find within, all that we need for life (I Cor 2:10–13).

The implication and challenge here for us is a deeper realization that we are not left on our own on this human sojourn. On the contrary, this outpouring of God's Spirit means that God can do infinitely more within us than we could ever imagine. The Spirit we have received is not a spirit of timidity but a Spirit of fire and passion, a Spirit that permeates all life, all creation, a Spirit of freedom that comes only to those who belong to God.

Were we able to grasp a tiny fragment of this mystery what implications would it bear upon us and our world? As mentioned earlier would we see ourselves and each other in a different light? Would it stop in the seeing or would we be serious in our efforts to treat ourselves and each other as God would treat us?

And what of our earth, the cosmos and all that is within it? Would we tread more lightly upon this earth? Would we co-exist with creation as though it were truly the sacred manifestation of God's glory or would we continue to dominate and conquer it?

If we believe that we too have received God's own Spirit then we are challenged to live from God's Spirit, to see with the eyes of God's Spirit, to relate to ourselves, each other and indeed all of creation as God relates. We are in effect, by virtue of God's Spirit within us, called to live as Jesus lived; to have the mind and heart of Jesus (1Cor 2:12–16).

Such is the depth of God's intimacy with us. Such is the longing in God to be one with us, to immerse us in God's own life.

4. HUMAN SUFFERING

In the face of human atrocities and suffering, what does Jesus' death, resurrection and the outpouring of God's Spirit say to those families, friends and nations who ache for the loss of innocent life? What does it say to all those who grieve and mourn for lives lost in massacres such as, Sarajevo and other war-torn countries; Oklahoma America, in the bombing that claimed over one hundred lives; Dunblane Scotland, in the school shooting which slaughtered little children and teachers, and in the senseless killings of tourists and workers in Port Arthur, Australia?

Where is the God of life and love and compassion in the midst of such human devastation? Has God forsaken those who suffer? Has the mystery and grace of Jesus' life, death and resurrection been wasted on the human heart that is broken and crippled by pain and anguish?

What sense, what meaning does the death, resurrection and the outpouring of Jesus' Spirit make in the lived reality of those who are oppressed and denied basic human dignity and freedom by corrupt power and injustice? Does God fail to see them as precious and honoured? What of those whose relationships fail, whose families fall apart, who exist in loneliness, who struggle with addiction, disabilities and illness, who are abused in their innocence and trust, who have fallen and despair; has God failed to uphold God's promise to be there (Jer 29:10–14)?

How do we reconcile a theology of God's indwelling and gracious love, of God's transcending and liberating grace with the everyday and extraordinarily absurd sufferings of the human spirit? I have no way of making sense in my own life, or in any other person's life, of a God who appears to abandon us in the depths of our sufferings, or worse still, a God, who some claim, instigates and causes us to suffer! The sense of God being the one who bears suffering down on us to teach us or punish us is utterly opposed to the God, who in Jesus, embraced our human suffering as one with us.

If we claim to believe in the God of Jesus then we are really challenged to review our understanding of human suffering and where God is in that suffering.

For most of us this requires a massive undoing of a theology that in essence contradicted the very nature of God and belied the very meaning of crucifixion and resurrection. To believe in the death and resurrection of Jesus is to seek God in our suffering in no other place than *with* us.

If we cannot find God in our suffering and struggling then surely it suggests we must be looking for God outside it, separate from it, in all the places where God will not be found for no other reason than the fact that God is *in the depths* of our suffering. The God of Jesus suffers with us, cries out with us and is broken with us or that God is not the God of Jesus.

Do we believe it? How do we know it? How do we live what we know to be true? Again, by virtue of the fact that I struggle with this so much in my own life, I have no answers. All there is for us, who are foolish enough in the eyes of this world to believe in Jesus, is the daily struggle to embrace our suffering with hearts and spirits that wrestle to open themselves to the mysterious ways of God's transcending grace.

This grace may come to us, paradoxically, in the words and deeds, in the touch and gestures of those who reach out and comfort us in our suffering. Or it may come to us simply in our human capacity to endure, to hope and to continue to seek life. The words of a young man whose wife was killed in the Port Arthur massacre, reveal something of this magnificent capacity in us. His words, "I/we will not allow evil to win", express so powerfully our unrelenting choice for life over death, for good over evil.

There is nothing magical about God being with us in our suffering. The external realities may never change or appear to be different. But when we experience within us a resilient spirit that gives us the courage to endure, or the strength to hold on, or the comforting peace that allows our weeping hearts to rest and wait, believing that hope will prevail over despair, darkness will be conquered by light and, in time, life will be renewed, then we know that God is truly with us in our suffering.

But to evade our suffering, to become embittered or twisted by it is to shut our spirits out from the very place where God longs to meet us and be one with us. That place is the sacred place where God's Presence and grace cradle what is bruised and broken in us, impoverished and aching, bringing forth from the refinement of grace upon our human mess, what God brought forth from the Cross of Jesus, a resurrected and transcendent spirit.

If we believe in the God of Jesus then we commit ourselves to the constant challenge of knowing, in a way that is beyond our knowing, that God does not break the crushed reed nor quench the wavering flame, but faithfully, reverently, in ways that at times we cannot see let alone understand, God brings about true justice and healing (Is 42:2–4).

5. EMMAUS—A MODEL FOR MINISTRY

As well as being a magnificent account of Jesus' Resurrection encounter with His disciples, the Emmaus story also provides us with an excellent model for our ministry. It brings together all the qualities of Jesus' ministry that we have been reflecting on. Let us consider them here, by way of bringing the threads of our reflection to closure.

In this Emmaus story we see how Jesus ministers to the disciples who make their journey from death to life, from confusion and doubt to conviction and faith. How does Jesus minister to them?

a) Jesus meets them where they are and as they are in the midst of their journey.

b) Jesus attends to them, by noticing how they are and inviting them to share their story.

c) Jesus listens to their story, becomes engaged in their reality.

d) Having connected with them Jesus responds to their story by sharing His own Christ story.

e) In sharing His story *in response to their story*, Jesus makes sense of their story; restores hope, gives new meaning and purpose.

f) Having connected with them, having shared their story and having responded with His own story, Jesus goes further; He meets their longing for more, He accepts their hospitality.

g) In an ordinary meal, in comm-union with them, He reveals Himself as the risen Christ.

h) Having fired their hearts He empowers them to return to the place of their dread with renewed spirits, with new vision, with a proclamation of new life!

Throughout these reflections we have been evaluating our lives and our ministry in light of how Jesus lived and ministered. Let us now, for the last time in this setting, consider what we do in our ministry.

a) Do we meet our people where they are and as they are?

b) Do we attend to their spirits, notice what is happening and acknowledge our awareness of that?

c) Do we listen to the story of our people?

d) Do we provide opportunities for them wherein Jesus' story can connect in some way with their story, or do we keep telling them the relevance of Jesus' story, unaware of their reality? Do we break open the Word *in response to and in relationship with their lives?*

e) Do we leave our people wanting more of the God we proclaim?

f) Do we accept from our people their gestures of hospitality, a smile, a word, a gesture, an invitation to listen or to share.

g) And in our comm-union with our people in the ordinary things of life, do they recognize the God of Jesus in us?

h) Do we provide our people with an opportunity to experience the burning in their hearts; the opportunity for them to experience the God of their longing?

i) Do we empower our people with renewed spirits, new vision and a proclamation of new life?

We have asked many questions and raised many issues. At the end of the day it is what we do in love that matters most, not the perfection of love, but the authenticity of our being in love.

Let us hold close to the One whose first loving of us empowers us and makes all good things of life possible in us. Let us go forth on our Emmaus journey, fired and impassioned with the Spirit of Jesus, so that we might embody as authentically as grace enables us, the God of Jesus whom we proclaim.

PART THREE: RESPONDING TO THE IMPLICATIONS

Personal synthesis:

1. What feelings do these reflections stir in you?

2. What issues and concerns do they raise for you?

3. What insights would you like to add to these reflections?

4. In what way do you live the Christian's "foolish wisdom"? What are the paradoxes you live within your own life? What sense do you make of them?

5. When have you experienced the Presence of God in the midst of your suffering? How did you know God was there? When have you felt the absence of God in your life? How did you experience that absence?

6. What does it mean to you to be referred to as the "temple of God" (I Cor 3:16–17)? How do you experience yourself as being graced by God's Spirit? What impact does this have on your daily living? How does it influence your ministry?

Scripture Reflection:

Take some quiet time to reflect on the following text.

The Road To Emmaus (Lk 24:13–35)

• Imagine yourself on this journey from the place of your own darkness. What would be weighing your spirit down? What would you be struggling to make sense of as you journey on?

• Imagine that Jesus meets you on your journey. How does He attend to you? What does He notice about you? What do you share of your story with Jesus?

• How does Jesus respond to your story? What sense does He make of your story? What meanings does He share with you?

Listen deeply, rest in the stillness as you listen now for the Word that gives meaning to your story. (Pause)

- When have you been left wanting more of God in your life?

   When have you felt a "burning in your heart" for the God for whom you long?

   Rest in that longing now.

For Group Sharing:

- Allow the group time to connect and gather before you begin discussing these questions. It is important to be aware of people's energy and readiness for what is to follow. In light of this, it may be more appropriate to be selective with these questions or even to disregard them and find another way for your group to respond to the implications.

1.   Each share in some way with the group something of your own personal synthesis of these reflections.

2.   What questions, concerns and issues do these reflections raise for you as a ministry team within your community?

3.   Share some of the paradoxes that you are aware of in your community? How are people dealing with them?

4.   Identify some of the difficult and painful situations in individuals' lives within your community. What are the questions of life and of God that are being raised in those situations? What image of God are you as a team presenting to those who are suffering in those situations? Are they experiencing the Presence of God in your support?

5.   What are the "resurrection" initiatives, programs and activities in your community? How are people experiencing the Spirit of the living God in and through your ministry?

6.   Reflect on the model of ministry Jesus gave us in the Emmaus story. In what way do you as a team honour this model? In what way can you integrate it more genuinely in your ministry?

7.   Take some time in quiet to discern how you move forward from this stage of your journey. Commit yourselves, in some way, to an initiative that will enable you to build on this sharing and to embody more faithfully the God you proclaim.

RITUAL AND PRAYER

It may be appropriate to mark this stage of your journey with a special Eucharistic liturgy. In planning and preparing for this liturgy it would be good to bring some of the threads of your sharing throughout this journey into the celebration.

Try to identify some element of each of your sharings that could be integrated into this liturgy, without overloading it.

Here are a few suggestions that may assist.

• Let the Emmaus story be the central theme of this liturgy.

Highlight it in some appropriate way as the Gospel for the liturgy. As well as this, give extra focus to the Fraction Rite, so that the breaking of the bread is highlighted, perhaps by a special hymn or by spot-light or by inviting the team to participate in the actual breaking up of the bread, as far as that is possible.

• Some of the following hymns may be helpful (please refer to page 191 for location of songs):
Song of God's People (ARH)
Come Holy Spirit (BUH)
Holy Sacred Spirit (ARH)
In Memory of You (ARH)
Shekinah (ARH)
A Remembering Heart (ARH)

Emmaus Song (COJ)
A New Dawn (BUH)

Conclude this liturgical celebration with a special meal to celebrate this time together.

ENDNOTES

Chapter 1

1. Sebastian Moore, *The Fire and the Rose Are One*, (London: Darton, Longman & Todd, 1980) 80.

2. Brian McDermott, quoted by Enda Lyons, *Jesus: Self-Portrait by God*, (Dublin: The Columba Press, 1994) 18.

3. Sebastian Moore, *The Crucified Is No Stranger*, (London: Darton, Longman & Todd, 1977) x.

Chapter 2

1. Karl Rahner, "The Spirituality of the Future". *The Practice of Faith: A Handbook of Contemporary Spirituality,* Lehmann, K.& Raffelt A.(eds) (London: SCM Press, 1985) 22.

2. T. Dunne, "Experience", *The New Dictionary of Catholic Spirituality,* Downey, M. (ed) (Collegeville, Minnesota: Liturgical Press, 1993) 366.

3. Karl Rahner, 22.

4. Ibid., 22.

Chapter 3

1. Pat O'Collins, *Intimacy and the Hungers of the Heart*, (Dublin: The Columba Press, 1991) 17.

2. Nicolas of Cusa, quoted Pat O'Collins ibid., 138.

3. Thomas Merton, quoted by J.Higgins, *Thomas Merton on Prayer*, (New York: Image Books, 1971) 59.

4. St. Augustine, *The Confessions of St. Augustine*, Sheed F.J., (London: Sheed & Ward, 1984) 1.

Chapter 4

1. Monica Brown, *In Image and Likeness: A Creative Approach to the Spirituality of Australian Catholic School Teachers,* (Unpublished thesis), Masters Honours, Australian Catholic University Strathfield, Sydney 1995, 72–73.

2. Rollo May, *The Courage to Create*, London: Collins, 1976) 39.

3. John Foley, *Creativity and the Roots of Liturgy*, (Washington: The Pastoral Press, 1994) 10.

4. H. Polanyi, *The Concept of Creativity in Science and Art*, Dutton D.& Krausz, M. (ed), (Boston: The Hage, 1981) 103.

5. Monica Brown, 73.

6. Pat O'Collins, 18.

7. Jill McCorquodale, *I Have Given You an Example: The Nature and Purpose of Ministry in the Light of the Ecclesiology of the Footwashing in the Gospel of John*. (Unpublished essay), Master of Arts in Pastoral Ministry, Boston College, 1993.

8. *Jerusalem Bible*, (London: Darton, Longman & Todd, 1966) 1116.

9. Monica Brown, 77.

10. Andrew Greeley, *Religious Imagination*, (Los Angeles: Sadlier, 1981) 10.

11. John Westerhoff, quoted by John Goodfellow, *Faith Education, Creativity and the Bicameral Mind*, (Catholic Primary Principles Association, 1986) 9.

12. Amos Wilder, *Theopoetic: Theology and Religious Imagination*, (Philadelphia: Fortress Press, 1976) 101.

13. Ibid., 2.

14. William Johnston, *The Cloud of Unknowing*, (New York: Image Books, 1973) 26.

15. Teilhard de Chardin, *Meditations With Teilhard de Chardin*, B. Gallagher (ed), (Santa Fe: Bear & Co, 1988) 31.

16. Mark Coleridge, "The Necessary Angel: Imagination and the Bible", *Pacifica*, Vol.1, No. 2, June 1988, 172.

17. William Bausch, *Storytelling: Imagination and Faith*, (Connecticut, Twenty-third Publications, 1985, 108.

18. St. Benedict, *RB 1980*, Timothy Fry (ed) (Collegeville, Minnesota: The Liturgical Press, 1981) 5.

Chapter 5

1. *Jerusalem Bible*, (London: Darton, Longman & Todd, 1966) 19.

2. Hildegard of Bingen, *Meditations with Hildegard of Bingen*, Gabriele Uhlein (ed) (Santa Fe: Bear & Co, 1983) 21.

3. Sebastian Moore, 1980, 20.

4. Juliana of Norwich, *Revelations of Divine Love*, (New York: Image Books, 1977) 88.

5. Mechtild of Magdeburg, *Meditations with Mechtild of Magdeburg*, Sue Woodruff (ed) (Santa Fe: Bear & Co 1982) 100.

Chapter 6

1. Tony Kelly, *The Way of Jesus*, (Unpublished)

2. Sebastian Moore, 1980, 80.

3. Sheila Cassidy, *Sharing the Darkness: The Spirituality Caring*, (London: of Darton, Longman & Todd, 1990) 11.

Chapter 7

1. Sebastian Moore, 1977, 4.

2. Sebastian Moore, 1980, 23.

4. Michael Lodahl, *Shekinah Spirit: Divine Presence in Jewish and Christian Religion*, (New York: Stimulus Book, 1992) 51–52.

5. Elizabeth Johnson, *She Who Is*, (New York: Crossroad, 1993) 86.

Music for the Soul

Monica Brown's Adult Music

The songs and hymns suggested for use in the ritual and prayer in part three of each chapter of this book, is original music by Monica Brown. The songs can be found in the following collections:

ALBUM	CODE
A Remembering Heart	(ARH)
Bring Us Home	(BUH)
God of My Life	(GOL)
Celebrating Our Journey	(COJ)
God Is...	(GI)

Monica's songs have been highly acclaimed both nationally and internationally, for their ability to touch the heart of the listener. They are musically appealing, inspired and grounded in scripture.

Songs such as A Remembering Heart, the Emmaus Song, Bring Us Home, My Plans for You, as well as the mantras, Gather Us O God, Holy Sacred Spirit, Healing is Your Touch and Lead Me Guide Me, have captured the hearts of many.

They are ideal for prayer and liturgy and are widely used in adult faith sharing. The songs are available on cassette and accompanying music book. If you would like further information or wish to order any of these collections please contact our office or complete the enclosed order form.

Australia & New Zealand:

Emmaus Productions, P.O. Box 54 Thornleigh, NSW, 2120 Australia
Phone (02) 9484 0252 Fax (02) 9481 9179

England, U.K. & Ireland:

St. Paul Multimedia, 199 Kensington High Street, London, W8 z6BA
Phone 0171 937 9591 Fax 0171 937 9910

USA & Canada:

Resource Publications, 160 E. Virginia Street #290, San Jose, Ca, 95112 5876 Phone 408 286 8505 Fax 408 287 8748

Monica also has published several collections of children's music for faith education, liturgy and prayer, which are available

 through the above outlets as well as major Christian book stores.

EMMAUS
PRODUCTIONS